acti✂ities
from the
Mathematics Teacher

Edited by

Evan M. Maletsky
Montclair State College
Upper Montclair, New Jersey

and

Christian R. Hirsch
Western Michigan University
Kalamazoo, Michigan

National Council of Teachers of Mathematics

Library of Congress Cataloging in Publication Data:

Main entry under title:

Activities from the Mathematics teacher.

  Bibliography: p.
  1. Mathematics--Study and teaching. I. Maletsky,
Evan M. II. Hirsch, Christian R. III. Mathematics
teacher.
QA11.A26   510'.7'12   81-4028
ISBN 0-87353-173-6   AACR2

Printed in the United States of America

Table of Contents

Introduction

The "Activities" section has been a regular feature of the *Mathematics Teacher* since 1972. The section provides classroom teachers and teacher educators with a useful source of discovery lessons, laboratory experiences, mathematical games and puzzles, and model constructions for use with students in grades 7 through 12. Each activity consists of a teacher's guide and three or four student worksheets designed to actively engage pupils in the process of *doing* mathematics. In some activities the worksheets can be used together, whereas in others they are more appropriately used one at a time. The activities can be used to stimulate, enhance, reinforce, or extend the learning of particular topics that appear in standard mathematics programs as well as to provide supplementary and enrichment experiences for individuals or small groups of students. In either situation, the use of the activities can contribute to the achievement of important process and affective goals in addition to specific content objectives. Specific objectives and teaching suggestions are given in the teacher's guide for each activity. However, teachers are encouraged to modify and adapt the worksheets to their own special interests and needs and their students' abilities.

This compilation of reprinted activities is organized in five sections around the following topics: computational skills, calculators, geometry, measurement, and problem solving. Space limitations prohibited the inclusion of all previously published activities. An annotated listing of additional topic-related activities that have appeared in the journal through December 1980 is therefore included at the end of each section.

The pages of this book are perforated so that they can be easily removed and reproduced for classroom use. We suggest that once an activity has been used, teachers keep the master and any additional copies in a file folder along with lesson plans for that particular unit. Teachers may wish to note possible adaptations or extensions of an activity on the teacher's guide as well.

Activities for
Computational Skills

Developing, mastering, and maintaining basic computational skills are among the goals of today's mathematics curriculum at all levels of learning from the primary grades through college. The classroom experiences designed to support these goals are numerous and diversified. The seven activities in this section reflect some approaches that are suitable for the middle and junior high school but readily adaptable to other levels as well.

The first two activities, "Magic Triangles" and "Foxy Fives," deal with the natural number skills. Each can be used over a wide range of abilities and can be counted on to be both motivating and challenging. "Manipulating Magic Squares" requires substantial numerical computation and can be useful in reviewing skills with whole numbers, integers, fractions, and decimals. The next activity, "Maintaining Computational Skills," suggests how the mathematics teacher can use a flowchart format on an overhead projector to produce many computational exercises. Especially suited for oral drill, it allows the teacher to review basic computational skills in a new and different format. The pace, difficulty level, and arithmetic operations can be widely varied.

The activity "Store Decimals" reviews basic skills with money—calculating bill totals and bank balances and writing checks—through various forms that are given to the student for completion. "Math Magic" provides arithmetic experiences that lead to the concept of a variable through a series of interesting and motivating mathematical "tricks." The section ends on a historical note with the activity "Ancient Babylonian Mathematics." The ingenious numeration system used by the Babylonians is studied first with the counting numbers and then with fractions. Valuable comparisons can be made with our own decimal system. The last worksheet describes an archaeological find that shows in striking fashion just how mathematically brilliant this civilization was some four thousand years ago.

For additional computational skills activities from the *Mathematics Teacher*, consult the annotated listing at the end of this section.

MAGIC TRIANGLES

By Janet Caldwell, Parkdale Collegiate, Toronto, Ontario

Teacher's Guide

Grade level: 7–10

Materials: One set of worksheets for each student; a transparency of each worksheet

Objectives: To provide computational practice; to enable the student to discover patterns and thereby make conjectures and generalizations

Directions: Distribute the activity sheets one at a time.

Sheet 1: After the students have completed sheet 1, make sure they understand the relationship among the side sum (s), the vertex sum (v), and the total sum of the digits used (t): $3s - v = t$. This pattern can be extended to sheets 2 and 3.

Sheet 2: The chart for sheet 2 can be completed immediately by using the formula $3s - v = t$ and the fact that $t = 45$. Note that solutions for $s = 18$ and $s = 22$ are not possible. Proof of this can be a supplementary activity.

Sheet 3: Again the chart can be completed immediately with the same formula and the fact that $t = 78$. Every triangle here has at least one solution as shown in table 1. By distributing the possibilities through-out the class, one can investigate the number of ways of completing each magic triangle.

TABLE 1

sum on each side	28	29	30	31	32	33	34	35	36	37
number of different magic triangles possible	1	3	7	12	15	15	12	7	3	1

Follow-up activity: If four spaces are to be filled between the vertices, how many magic triangles would be expected? How many magic triangles would be expected if there are n spaces between the vertices?

REFERENCES

Carmony, Lowell A. "A Minimathematical Problem: The Magic Triangles of Yates." *Mathematics Teacher* 70 (May 1977): 410–13.

Sharp, J. Norman C. "Polygonal Numbergrams." *Ontario Mathematics Gazette* 15 (March 1976): 21–24.

Yates, Daniel S. "Magic Triangles and a Teacher's Discovery." *Arithmetic Teacher* 23 (May 1976): 351–54.

Editorial comment: These activities put a review of basic computational skills in the context of a discovery situation. Students look for numerical solutions by trial and error, search for patterns, make conjectures, and then attempt to generalize. Don't hurry through the activities but rather give the students time to explore and test their own ideas. Don't deprive them of the challenge and excitement that come from making their own discoveries.

Using the numbers 1,2,3,4,5, and 6, fill in the circles so
that the sum along each side is equal to the number given
below the diagram. Each digit is to be used exactly once.

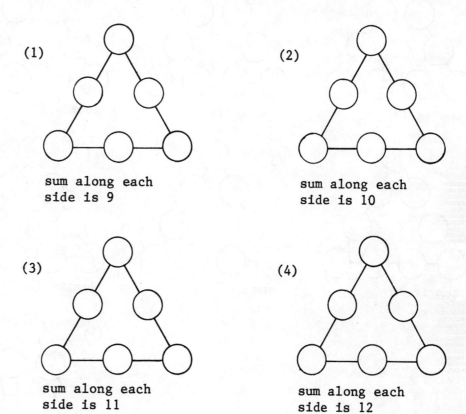

(1)

sum along each
side is 9

(2)

sum along each
side is 10

(3)

sum along each
side is 11

(4)

sum along each
side is 12

Complete the following chart:

sum along each side (s)	9	10	11	12
sum of the vertices (v)				
3s – v				

What is the sum (t) of the digits used in each triangle?

Using the numbers 1 through 9, fill in the circles so that
the sum along each side is the same as that given below the
diagram. Be careful here, since two triangles have no solutions.

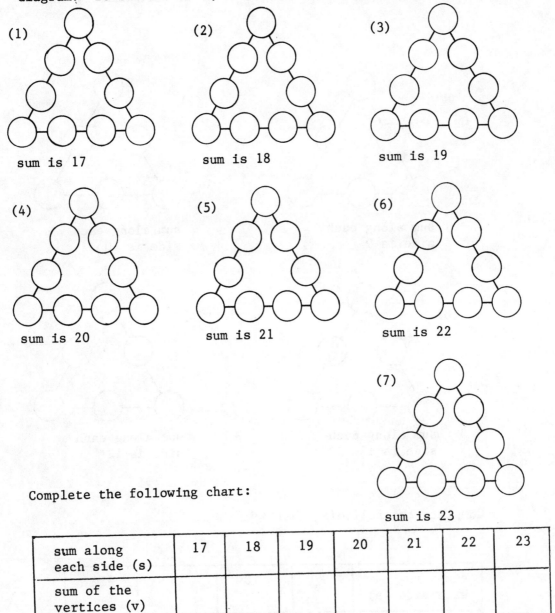

(1)

sum is 17

(2)

sum is 18

(3)

sum is 19

(4)

sum is 20

(5)

sum is 21

(6)

sum is 22

(7)

sum is 23

Complete the following chart:

sum along each side (s)	17	18	19	20	21	22	23
sum of the vertices (v)							
3s – v							

What is the sum (t) of the digits used?

Complete the following magic triangles using the numbers
1 through 12. All triangles have at least one solution.

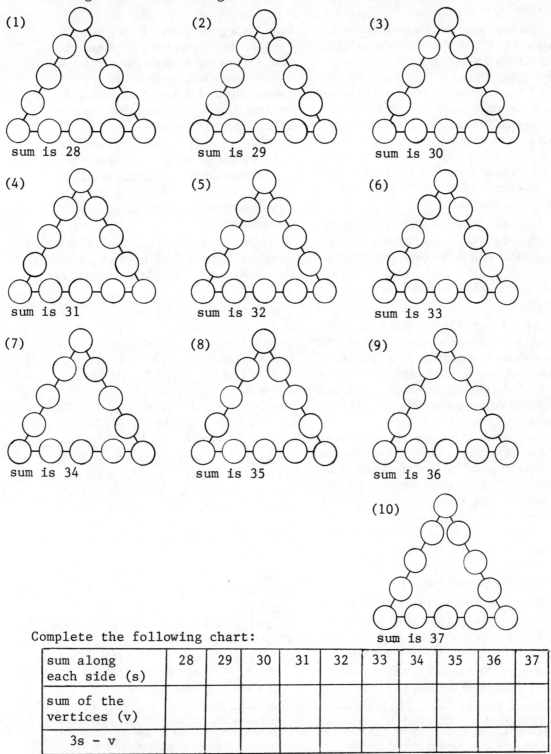

(1) sum is 28

(2) sum is 29

(3) sum is 30

(4) sum is 31

(5) sum is 32

(6) sum is 33

(7) sum is 34

(8) sum is 35

(9) sum is 36

(10) sum is 37

Complete the following chart:

sum along each side (s)	28	29	30	31	32	33	34	35	36	37
sum of the vertices (v)										
3s – v										

What is the sum (t) of the digits used?

FOXY FIVES

By Vicki Schell, Salzburg International Preparatory School, Salzburg, Austria

Grade Levels: 7–12

Materials: One set of activity sheets and one deck of Foxy Five cards per student. To make a deck of cards, cut sixty-two $2\frac{1}{4}$-by-$3\frac{1}{2}$-inch rectangles from posterboard (or for a thinner card, cut from a three-by-five-inch file card; blank card decks are also commercially available). Mark three cards with the number "1," three with the number "2," continuing through "10"; mark each number from 11 through 17 on two cards each; and for numbers 18 through 25, mark one card each.

Objectives: To provide experience in observing the relationships among numbers; to provide drill in the basic arithmetic operations; and to provide experience in applying the order of operations to a set of numbers

Background: Playing the Foxy Fives game is my foxy way of sneaking in drill and review to general mathematics classes. The deck consists of cards numbered from 1 to 25. Each player is dealt five cards, and one card is turned up in the center. The object of the game is to combine the five cards in any order and, using any of the four basic operations, to obtain the number on the center card. The students should be familiar with the basic game before trying any variations. As an alternative approach, these activities can be done without cards by selecting the numbers in some random procedure (using a spinner is such an option), but the students seem to find it easier having the cards at hand.

Directions: Distribute the card decks and activity sheets (one at a time) to each student. Have the students complete each sheet before going on to the next one.

Sheet 1: This initial activity familiarizes the students with the basic procedure of the Foxy Fives game. It may be helpful to do this sheet as a class group, using an overhead, the first few times the game is played. It is interesting to compare results of different students as a means of reinforcing the fact that there is often more than one possible solution to a problem.

Sheets 2 & 3: These sheets reinforce the discovery that the same Foxy Five numbers will produce a different total depending on how the numbers are combined, as well as providing additional practice in number manipulation.

Solution Guide: There are, of course, many possible solutions for each of the given problems. I include here one solution for each.

Sheet 1: (1) $10 - (6 + 3 + 1) + 5 = 5$; (2) $11 + 1 - 9 - (8 \div 8) = 2$; (3) $11 - [(20 - 15) \times 3 - 10] = 6$; (4) $(11 + 3) - 12 + 18 - 12 = 8$; (5) $(4 + 16) \div 10 - (25 - 24) = 1$; (6) $17 - 17 + (14 - 13) \times 7 = 7$; (7) $(9 - 9) + (5 \times 4) + 2 = 22$; (8) $(7 - 6) + [3 - (10 \div 5)] = 2$; (9) $5 - [(11 + 21) \div 8] + 6 = 7$; (10) $(17 - 1) \div [(6 - 2) \div 2] = 8$; (11) $(10 + 1) - 11 + (9 - 4) = 5$.

Sheet 2: (2) $9 - \{14 \div [(19 + 3) \div 11]\} = 2$; (3) $11 - [(19 + 9) \div 14] \div 3 = 3$; (4) $19 - 9 + 11 - 14 - 3 = 4$; (5) $9\{14 - [(11 + 19) \div 3]\} = 5$; (7) $14 \div \{[(3 + 19) - 9] - 11\} = 7$; (8) $9 - [(11 \times 3) \div (14 + 19)] = 8$; (9) $11 \times 3 - (14 + 19) + 9 = 9$; (10) $19 - 9 + 11 - 14 + 3 = 10$.

Sheet 3: (1) $[(11 + 3) - (2 \times 7)] \div 5 = 0$; (2) $[(2 \times 5) + (7 - 3)] - 11 = 3$; (3) $5 - [(11 + 3) \div 7 + 2] = 1$; (4) $[(5 + 3) - (11 - 7)] \div 2 = 2$; (5) $[(5 + 3) \div (11 - 7)] \times 2 = 4$; (6) $2 \times 3 \times 5 \times 7 \times 11 = 2310$; (7) $11 \times 7 \times 5 \times (3 + 2) = 1925$; (8) $[(11 - 3) \times (5 + 7)] \div 2 = 48$; (9) $5 - \{3 - [(11 - 2) - 7]\} = 4$; (10) $11 \times 7 \times 5 \times 3 - 2 = 1153$.

Editorial comment: This activity can generate a great deal of interest while at the same time offering substantial review of basic operations with the natural numbers. In a classroom setting, it can be used individually, with groups, or with all students competing in teams. Encourage speed in doing the trial mental computations. Be sure to take the time to have students express and write their own diversified solutions, of which there will be many. Use the errors made to emphasize the basic arithmetic facts and skills and to identify common sources of mistakes. A valuable follow-up is to have selected students explain the strategies they developed and used in solving the Foxy Fives problems.

FOXY FIVES

Directions:

- Deal yourself the following Foxy Five hands. Use each card once (and only once) to make the given total.

- Write out your combination, being sure to introduce parentheses where needed to show the order of operations.

Example:

hand: 7, 8, 1, 9, 9   total: 16 $(9 \div 9) \times (7 + 8 + 1) = 16$

1. 1, 5, 3, 6, 10   total: 5   _____

2. 8, 11, 9, 1, 8   total: 2   _____

3. 11, 10, 15, 20, 3   total: 6   _____

4. 12, 18, 3, 11, 12   total: 8   _____

5. 4, 16, 10, 24, 25   total: 1   _____

6. 17, 14, 7, 17, 13   total: 7   _____

7. 2, 9, 5, 9, 4   total: 22   _____

8. 3, 6, 10, 5, 7   total: 2   _____

9. 8, 6, 11, 5, 21   total: 7   _____

10. 6, 1, 2, 2, 17   total: 8   _____

11. 10, 4, 1, 11, 9   total: 5   _____

FOXY FIVES

Directions:

- Deal yourself the following Foxy Fives hand: 11, 14, 3, 19, 9.

- With this hand, make the totals from 1 to 11. Write each combination as an equation. Be careful of the order of operations!

1. $(11 + 14 - 19 + 3) \div 9 = 1$

2. _____

3. _____

4. _____

5. _____

6. $11 - [(19 + 9) \div 14 + 3] = 6$

7. _____

8. _____

9. _____

10. _____

11. $[9 - (19 - 14) - 3] \times 11 = 11$

FOXY FIVES

Directions:

- Deal yourself the following Foxy Fives hand: 2, 3, 5, 7, 11. (Notice that these are the first 5 prime numbers!)
- With this hand, find the following totals. Write each combination as an equation. Be careful of the order of operations!

1. What is the smallest whole number that you can find, using these five numbers and each arithmetic operation exactly once?

   _____

2. Find the smallest odd prime number. _____

3. Find the smallest odd natural number. _____

4. Find the smallest prime number. _____

5. Find the smallest composite natural number. _____

6. What is the largest composite natural number you can find?

   _____

7. What is the largest odd natural number you can find?

   _____

8. Find the largest even natural number possible, using each operation

   only once. _____

9. Find a natural number using only subtraction. _____

   _____

10. Find the largest prime number possible with these five numbers.

   _____

MANIPULATING MAGIC SQUARES

December 1972

By Evan M. Maletsky, Montclair State College, Upper Montclair, NJ 07043

Teacher's Guide

Grade level: 7, 8, and 9

Materials: One set of worksheets for each student. Transparency of magic square shown on next page.

Objectives: To recognize the various results of rotating and flipping over a square array of numbers (Sheet 1). To develop increased arithmetic competency using fractions and decimals (Sheet 2). To develop computational skills with integers (Sheet 3).

Directions: Distribute a set of worksheets to each student.

MAGIC SQUARES Sheet 1: Complete with the students the first magic square. Then show how a transparency of the original magic square can be flipped about its vertical axis to form a new magic square in this position. Now have the students complete the rest of the magic squares. Let them show how the transparency can be moved into each of these other positions by rotations and flips. In all, eight positions are possible.

MAGIC SQUARES Sheet 2: Have the students complete each new magic square and record the sum of the numbers in every row, column, and diagonal. Discuss why another magic square is always formed from operations of this type.

MAGIC SQUARES Sheet 3: Review the rules for operations with integers. Then have the students complete each new magic square.

Supplementary Activities: Show a method for constructing odd-ordered magic squares. Then have your students prepare a 5 × 5 magic square.

REFERENCES

Andrews, W. S. *Magic Squares and Cubes.* New York: Dover Publications, 1960. P. 199.

Gardner, Martin. *Mathematical Puzzles and Diversions,* Books 1 and 2. New York: Simon & Schuster, 1959 and 1961. Book 1, pp. 130–40; Book 2, pp. 15–22.

Kraitchik, Maurice. *Mathematical Recreations.* New York: W. W. Norton, 1942. Pp. 142–92.

Editorial comment: Numerous modifications of these magic-square activities can be made to offer additional practice on basic computational skills. Have your students transform a magic square by finding a given percent of each entry or by dividing each entry by a counting number and simplifying each resulting value. Transformations can be made to produce entries that are mixed numbers. Any linear transformation $ax + b$ on a magic square forms another magic square. If you start with a 3 × 3 magic square with row, column, and diagonal sum S, then the sum for the new magic square will be $aS + 3b$.

This array of numbers is a 3 x 3 MAGIC SQUARE.
Show that the sum of the numbers in each row,
column, and diagonal is 15.

8	1	6
3	5	7
4	9	2

Complete these magic squares using the same numbers 1 through 9. Be sure
each row, column, and diagonal adds to 15.

6		8
		4

4		
	9	
	7	

2	9	
7		

8		4
	7	

6		
	3	4

4		
	5	
	1	

Describe how to move the original magic square
into the six positions shown above.

Can you find another magic square using the
same numbers 1 through 9?

Can you find still another?

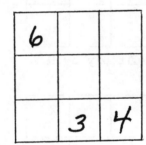

This array of numbers is a 3 x 3 MAGIC SQUARE. Show that the sum of the numbers in each row, column, and diagonal is 12.

7	0	5
2	4	6
3	8	1

Perform the indicated operations on each number in the magic square above. Enter the results below. Then see if each new array is also a magic square.

Add 9

Multiply by 12

Multiply by 150

Add 1.6

Multiply by 0.7

Multiply by 2.5

Add 3/4

Multiply by 3/4

Multiply by 2 1/4

If the same number is added to each entry in a magic square, is the result another magic square? How is the sum of the numbers in each row, column, and diagonal related to the original sum of 12?

If each entry in a magic square is multiplied by the same number, is the result another magic square? How is the sum of the numbers in each row, column, and diagonal related to the original sum of 12?

NAME _____

This array of numbers is a 3 x 3 MAGIC SQUARE.
Show that you get the same sum when you add
the numbers in each row, column, and diagonal.

Perform the indicated operations on each number in the magic square above. Enter the results below. Then see if each new array is
also a magic square.

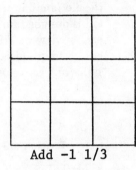

3	-4	1
-2	0	2
-1	4	-3

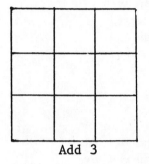

Add 3

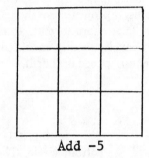

Add -5

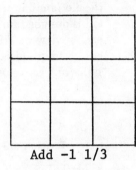

Add -1 1/3

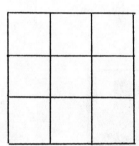

Subtract 5

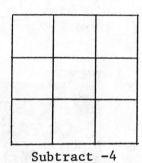

Subtract -4

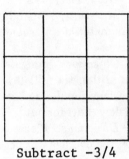

Subtract -3/4

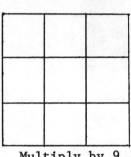

Multiply by 9

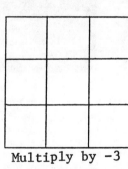

Multiply by -3

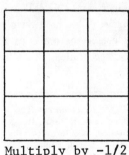

Multiply by -1/2

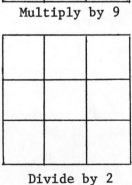

Divide by 2

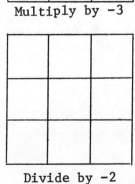

Divide by -2

Divide by -1/3

MAINTAINING COMPUTATIONAL SKILLS

April 1975

By Evan M. Maletsky, Montclair State College, Upper Montclair, NJ 07043

A real challenge facing mathematics teachers today is the maintenance and improvement of their students' computational skills. One approach to this problem centers on the format of presentation. Students need to see the old familiar problems of arithmetic in new and varied ways. This activity aid is designed for use on the overhead projector by the teacher. It can serve as a review of skills through the flow chart format. It is simple to make, easily adaptable to many ability levels, readily modified to stress specific skills, and convenient to use for rapidly paced oral drill.

Teacher's Guide

Grade level: 7–9

Materials: A manila file folder or similar material and some strips of clear acetate

Objective: Students will gain practice in arithmetic skills by finding outputs for various input numbers and operations in a flow chart format.

Directions: Place the completed chart on the overhead projector as shown in the photograph. The first strip is used to select an INPUT number for the top circle. The next two strips are used to select a sequence of OPERATIONS for the rectangles. The students then compute the resulting OUTPUT number for the bottom circle. The strips on Sheet 1 are for review with decimals, and those on Sheet 2 review fractions.

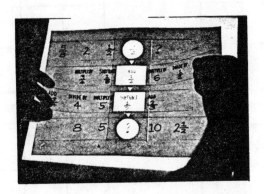

Editorial comment: This activity gives the teacher an aid to use as part of a continuing program of maintenance of basic skills. It can be used at the beginning of class as a rapid-fire five-minute review in mental computation, as a form for a quiz, as an extended, methodical summary, or in various other ways. The format lends itself to a wide choice of adaptations including a review of place value, rounding, use of parentheses, percents, powers and roots, simple algebraic expressions, and the like. A flowchart with only one operation can be used for slower classes, whereas three operation strips can be employed for faster classes.

Construction:

1. Cut an $8\frac{1}{2}$ by 11 inch sheet from a manila file folder or comparable material.

2. Hold the sheet horizontally, copying these figures full size down the center.

3. With a sharp knife or razor blade cut out the circles, rectangles, and small arrowheads.

4. Next cut the eight slots as marked. Make each slot $1\frac{1}{2}$ inches long.

5. Reproduce directly the two sets of strips of acetate as shown on Sheets 1 and 2. Cut each strip $1\frac{3}{8}$ inches wide.

6. Insert the strips in their appropriate slots so that they are under the cutouts but above the base elsewhere. You should be able to see all entries but only those under the cutouts will be projected.

Use:

1. Begin with an input number and two simple operations. Have the student compute the output. Vary the input number next, and then select other operations. Move quickly to those at the appropriate level.

2. For each sequence have the students write the corresponding mathematical expression. Then give other appropriate expressions and have the students select the correct input and operations on the flow chart.

3. Reading up in the reverse order, use an output number and the inverse operations to compute the correct input.

Extension:

1. Make additional strips of acetate for use with whole numbers and percents.

2. Practice writing equations by using the variable x as an input in the flow chart.

3. Show how an equation can be solved by reversing the flow chart and using the inverse operations.

References:

Morrow, Lorna J. "Flow Charts for Equation Solving and Maintenance Skills." MATHEMATICS TEACHER 66 (October 1973): 499-506.

Sobel, Max A., and Evan M. Maletsky. Teaching Mathematics: A Sourcebook of Aids, Activities, and Strategies. Englewood Cliffs, N.J.: Prentice-Hall, 1975.

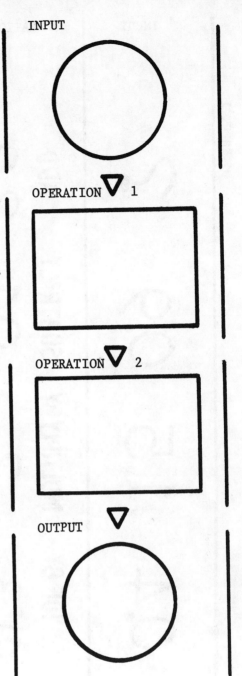

INPUT

OPERATION 1

OPERATION 2

OUTPUT

INPUT	OPERATION 1	OPERATION 2	OUTPUT
?	ADD 3.2	DIVIDE BY 3	9.6
0.9	SUBTRACT 0.1	MULTIPLY BY 6	10
1.5	MULTIPLY BY 2	ADD 0.5	?
0.4	DIVIDE BY 0.3	SUBTRACT 0.2	8
18	ADD 7	MULTIPLY BY 1.6	12

INPUT	OPERATION 1	OPERATION 2	OUTPUT
?	DIVIDE BY $\frac{1}{2}$	ADD $\frac{2}{3}$	$2\frac{1}{2}$
$\frac{3}{4}$	MULTIPLY BY 6	SUBTRACT $\frac{1}{2}$	10
$\frac{1}{2}$	ADD $\frac{1}{4}$	MULTIPLY BY 5	?
2	SUBTRACT $\frac{1}{8}$	DIVIDE BY 4	5
$\frac{5}{8}$	MULTIPLY BY $\frac{3}{4}$	ADD $1\frac{3}{4}$	8

INPUT	OPERATION 1	OPERATION 2	OUTPUT

STORE DECIMALS

By Kenneth J. Wundrow, Loyal Junior High School—Loyal, WI 54446

Teacher's Guide

Grade level: 7–12

Materials: Copies of worksheets 1–4; bank balance slips

Objectives: The students will calculate bill totals, complete checks and check stubs, and determine the bank balance.

Directions: The object of this game is to adjust the store bills so that the bank balance is as close to $0.00 as possible. Duplicate all materials and distribute them as a packet. On slips of paper, write bank totals that range from $275.00 to $475.00. The amounts must end in combinations of nickels or dimes in order to complete this activity successfully. Students should select a bank balance at random.

Rules: Explain the following rules to the students:

Step 1: Each student should compute the totals for each of the nine store bills. For each item where the quantity is left blank, a 1 should be placed at this time.

Step 2: The students should select six store bills in which the grand total is less than their bank total.

Step 3: Students may now change the number of items that had been left blank originally. They may change their number of items to any amount between 1 and 5. They should then recalculate the total of each bill and the grand total, trying to obtain a grand total equal to their bank balance. (Students may adjust the number of items several times in order to obtain the grand total closest to their bank balance.)

Step 4: Finally, students write a check to each of the six stores for the total on that bill and complete the check stubs. The student who has a bank balance closest to $0.00 is the winner.

Note: Students could use a hand calculator to check their work prior to handing in their material.

Editorial comment: For this activity each student will need one copy of sheets 1–3 and two copies of sheet 4. After a unit on percents, this activity could be modified to include the calculation of tax, say at 4 percent, on totals to obtain total amounts due. Another possible related activity is to have pupils complete an order form from a catalog store so that the total bill (including shipping and tax) is as close to a specified amount as possible.

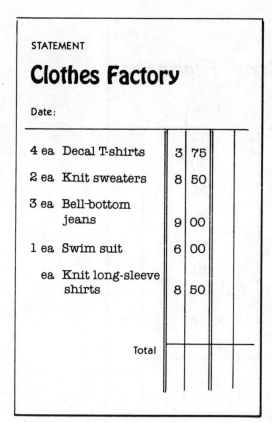

STATEMENT

Clothes Factory

Date:

4 ea	Decal T-shirts	3	75
2 ea	Knit sweaters	8	50
3 ea	Bell-bottom jeans	9	00
1 ea	Swim suit	6	00
ea	Knit long-sleeve shirts	8	50
	Total		

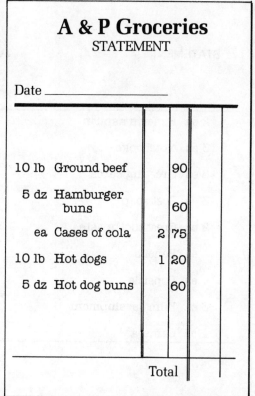

A & P Groceries
STATEMENT

Date _____

10 lb	Ground beef		90
5 dz	Hamburger buns		60
ea	Cases of cola	2	75
10 lb	Hot dogs	1	20
5 dz	Hot dog buns		60
	Total		

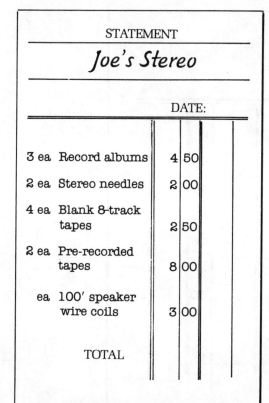

STATEMENT

Joe's Stereo

DATE:

3 ea	Record albums	4	50
2 ea	Stereo needles	2	00
4 ea	Blank 8-track tapes	2	50
2 ea	Pre-recorded tapes	8	00
ea	100' speaker wire coils	3	00
	TOTAL		

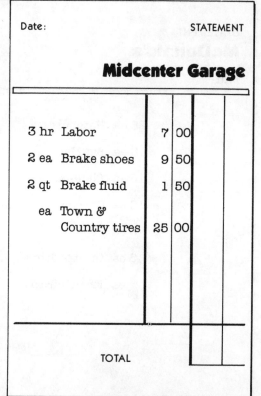

Date: STATEMENT

Midcenter Garage

3 hr	Labor	7	00
2 ea	Brake shoes	9	50
2 qt	Brake fluid	1	50
ea	Town & Country tires	25	00
	TOTAL		

Rexall Pharmacy

STATEMENT

Date:

2 ea	Bufferin aspirin		70
3 ea	Notebooks		60
5 ea	Greeting cards		35
3 ea	Zest soap		30
2 ea	Crest toothpaste		90
ea	Pencils		05
ea	Popsicle		10
3 ea	Film development	3	50
1 ea	Camera	25	00

TOTAL

McDonald's

STATEMENT

DATE:

25 ea	Hamburgers	25
10 ea	Big Macs	75
15 ea	Cheeseburgers	40
10 ea	Chocolate shakes	60
5 ea	Pepsi	25
5 ea	Orange drink	25
ea	French fries	30

Total

Coop Center

STATEMENT			Date:			
3 gl	Interior latex paint	9	00		
2 gl	Exterior latex paint	10	00		
3 ea	Paint brushes	3	50		
	lb Nails		50		
20 ea	8' building studs	1	10		
1 ea	Aluminum ladder	33	00		
	TOTAL				

STATEMENT

Athlete Store

DATE:

5 ea	Mag baseball bats	10	00		
3 ea	Baseballs	3	50		
8 ea	Hockey sticks	2	50		
2 ea	Spalding XO-9 footballs	12	75		
	ea Voit volleyballs	8	75		
	TOTAL				

Northwest Fabrics

STATEMENT			DATE:	
4 yd	Solid Double Knit	4.00		
	yd Denim	1.25		
4 cd	Buttons	.60		
3 sp	Thread	.50		
5 ea	Needles	.40		
4 ea	Patterns	1.25		
1 yd	Leather	10.00		
	TOTAL			

MATH MAGIC

By Miriam A. Leiva, University of North Carolina at Charlotte, Charlotte, NC 28223

Teacher's Guide

Grade level: 7–10

Materials: One set of worksheets for each student. Calculators would be helpful for sheet 3.

Objectives: To generate interest in mathematics while providing arithmetical experiences that lead to the introduction of the concept of a variable

Directions: Distribute copies of the activity sheets, one at a time, to each student. Sheet 1 may be used independently of the other sheets to provide self-checking computational practice by having pupils complete the tricks using additional numbers, perhaps including fractions. You may wish to indicate that using many numbers to verify a trick does not, however, assure us that it will *always* work. Sheet 2 introduces the notion of a variable as a means to discover why the tricks work as they do. Within this context, a variable is simply a symbol used to denote any one of a given set of numbers. Sheet 3 provides opportunities for pupils to exercise a little "magic" of their own. They should be encouraged to verify their tricks using numbers and then to show that they will always work by using a variable. The final trick on this sheet should convince students that an under-standing of the use of variables is not sufficient, however, for removing all the magic from mathematics. Numbers, other than powers of 2, frequently produce long sequences of results. For example, the choice of the number 9 produces a sequence of eighteen results before a 1 is obtained. Pupils who have had an introduction to computer programming should be encouraged to write a program that will carry out the instructions. This will expedite the testing of more and larger numbers. An analysis of the output will yield some interesting patterns. A discussion of some of these patterns may be found in Nievergelt, Farrar, and Reingold (1974).

Answers: 1. The result will always be the number chosen.　2. The result of this trick will always be 2.　3. The result will always be 6.　4. n, $3n$, $3n + 8$, $4n + 8$, $n + 2$, 2; n, $2n + 1$, $2n + 12$, $n + 6$, 6.　5. Subtract 18; divide by 3.　6. Answers will vary.　7. It is an unproved conjecture that the instructions will always produce a 1.

REFERENCE

Nievergelt, J., J. C. Farrar, and E. M. Reingold. *Computer Approaches to Mathematical Problems.* Englewood Cliffs, N.J.: Prentice-Hall, 1974.

Editorial comment: To set the stage for this activity you might perform a little "math magic" to guess the birthday of a few of your students. Have each student write the number of her or his month of birth (use 1 for January, 2 for February, and so on); multiply by 5; add 6; multiply by 4; add 9; multiply by 5; and then add the number of the day of birth. Ask a few students for the results of their computation. By subtracting 165 from their number you will obtain a three- or four-digit number that tells you the month and day of birth. For example, if the number is 1005, the birthday is October 5. Many pupils should be able to explain this trick after completing the activity.

Activities from the *Mathematics Teacher* 　23

Recently I found myself in the company of Matt-E-Magic, a skillful
magician. He involved me in some interesting math magic tricks, some
of which I want to share with you.

1.   INSTRUCTIONS   NUMBER CHOICES

          Choose any number   5   12   36   81

          Multiply by 2   10 _____

          Add 5   15 _____

          Multiply by 5   75 _____

          Subtract 25   50 _____

          Divide by 10   5 _____

   a. Follow Matt-E-Magic's instructions for the numbers 12, 36, and
       81 above. Write each step as in the example.

   b. Suppose the magician's instructions were carried out for a
       decimal, such as 0.62. What do you think the final result
       would be? Carry out the instructions and test your prediction.

   c. Do you think the result of this magical trick will always be
       the number chosen?

2.   INSTRUCTIONS   NUMBER CHOICES

          Choose any number   9   22   -5   0.3

          Multiply by 3   27 _____

          Add 8   35 _____

          Add your original   44 _____
          number choice

          Divide by 4   11 _____

          Subtract your original   2 _____
          number choice

   a. Follow Matt-E-Magic's instructions for the other numbers, 22,
       -5, and 0.3.

   b. Will the result of this magical trick always be 2? Check it
       one more time with a number of your choice.

3.   <u>INSTRUCTIONS</u>   <u>NUMBER CHOICES</u>

Choose any number   14   30   −7   0.4

Add the number one larger than   29
your original number choice

Add 11   40

Divide by 2   20

Subtract your original   6
number choice

a.   Follow Matt-E-Magic's instructions for the numbers 30, −7, and
     0.4.

b.   Do you think the result of this magical trick will always be
     6? Check it one more time using a number of your choice.

What is the secret behind these math magic tricks?

To find out, let us reconsider the first trick on sheet 1. Suppose
we refer to the number chosen as "number," or more simply as just <u>n</u>.

Choose any number	number	$\underline{n}$
Multiply by 2	2(number)	$2\underline{n}$
Add 5	2(number) + 5	$2\underline{n} + 5$
Multiply by 5	10(number) + 25	$10\underline{n} + 25$
Subtract 25	10(number)	$10\underline{n}$
Divide by 10	number	$\underline{n}$

Aha! Now it is easy to see why the magic works. Since "number" or <u>n</u>
can represent any particular choice of number, the result must always
be the original number.

4.   Discover the magic behind tricks 2 and 3 by using the word
     "number" or the letter <u>n</u> for the number chosen in each case.
     Write each step on a separate line as was done above.

Now it is your turn to work some magic.

5. Each of the math magic tricks below is missing one instruction.
   Fill in the instruction so that, in each case, the result will
   always be the original number chosen.

INSTRUCTIONS	INSTRUCTIONS
Choose any number	Choose any number
Multiply by 4	Multiply by 2
Add 6	Add 9
Multiply by 3	Add your original number choice
_____	_____
Divide by 12	Subtract 3

6. Make up a math magic trick in which the final result will always
   be 7, no matter what number is chosen.

7. Your experiences in this activity have dispelled much of the magic
   in Matt-E-Magic's program. However, he concluded his performance
   with the following trick, which I have yet to unravel.

INSTRUCTIONS

1. Choose any whole number other than 0.
2. a. If the number is even, divide by 2 and then
      carry out instruction 3.
   b. If the number is odd, multiply by 3, add 1, and
      then carry out instruction 3.
3. a. If your result is 1, stop.
   b. If your result is not 1, repeat instruction 2
      using your result as the number.

Example: If your number choice is 5, the sequence of results is
          $5 \rightarrow 16 \rightarrow 8 \rightarrow 4 \rightarrow 2 \rightarrow 1$ (stop).

No one in the audience could find a number for which the instructions
did not eventually produce a 1. Can you?

ANCIENT BABYLONIAN MATHEMATICS

By Evan M. Maletsky, Montclair State College, Upper Montclair, NJ 07043

Teacher's Guide

Grade level: 7–12

Materials: One set of worksheets per student

Objectives: Babylonian mathematics flourished in ancient Mesopotamia, between the Tigris and Euphrates rivers. Wedge-shaped writing called cuneiform was recorded by making impressions in clay tablets. Thousands of these tablets have been uncovered by archaeologists, and in recent years some of their mysteries have been unraveled. This activity is designed to help students explore one of these archaeological finds, which is now located in the Yale Babylonian Collection 7289, and to help them gain an appreciation for the high level of mathematics that had developed in this part of the world nearly four thousand years ago.

Directions: Have the students do the worksheets one at a time. Class discussion and review should follow the completion of each sheet.

Sheet 1: Emphasize the use of powers of 60 as place values and relate it to the use of powers of 10 in our own decimal system. *Answers:*

1. (13) <vvv (35) $\begin{matrix} < \\ < \end{matrix}$ vvv (51) $\begin{matrix} < \\ < \end{matrix}$ v
2. (257)c   (1000)a   (1976)b
3. 10 000

Sheet 2: Again, relate their fractions with powers of 60 as denominators to our decimal place values.

Decimal place values

$$\ldots 10^3 \; 10^2 \; 10^1 \; 1 \; \frac{1}{10^1} \; \frac{1}{10^2} \; \frac{1}{10^3} \ldots$$

Babylonian place values

$$\ldots 60^3 \; 60^2 \; 60^1 \; 1 \; \frac{1}{60^1} \; \frac{1}{60^2} \; \frac{1}{60^3} \ldots$$

Use question 4 to show the important role our decimal point plays, and how confusing it would be if we, like the Babylonians, could not differentiate among, say, 36, 3.6, and 0.36 in our numeration system.

Answers:

1. 15/60, 25/60; 18/60, 21/60; 36/60, 58/60
2. 45/60, 33/60, 54/60
3. 141/200 = 0.705
4. 3258, 54.3, 0.905

Sheet 3: Encourage careful computation by the students. If possible, have a hand-held calculator available for use. The students should draw the correct conclusion that the Babylonians had a very accurate estimate of $\sqrt{2}$ and that they knew the diagonal relationship for a square. Note that this was some twelve-hundred years before Pythagoras. *Answers:*

2. 0.416666, 0.009722; 42.426388
3. 0.400000, 0.014166, 0.000046; 1.414212
4. 42.4263
5. yes

REFERENCES

Aaboe, Asger. *Episodes from the Early History of Mathematics.* New York: L. W. Singer Co., 1964.

Neugebauer, Otto. *The Exact Sciences of Antiquity.* New York: Dover Publications, 1969.

Editorial comment: The three worksheets in this activity are written at different levels of difficulty. For lower-level classes, use only the first worksheet, which discusses place value and powers of 60 and gives a review of computation with whole numbers in an interesting and different format. Contrast this system with the familiar Roman numeration system. The second worksheet will give an average class more review of computational skills as well as an insight into the role of place value in fractions. It also shows why the decimal point and the digit 0 are essential in our own decimal system of numeration to avoid possible ambiguities. Upper-level classes will enjoy exploring and discussing the significance of the Babylonian tablet described in worksheet 3. Interested students should be encouraged to explore other ancient systems of numeration, including those of the Egyptians, Greeks, and Mayans.

The Babylonians wrote their numerals in cuneiform fashion with wedge-shaped characters impressed on clay tablets.

1. Two basic symbols were used.
    The vertical symbol represented 1 unit.   V - one unit
    The horizontal symbol represented 10 units.   < - ten units

Study these examples.	Then try these
24 ⟨ VVVV	13
42 ⟨⟨ VV	35
30 ⟨	51

2. To represent numbers larger than 60, another position with a place value of 60 was added.

$$\underbrace{\text{VV}} \quad \underbrace{⟨V}$$

2 <u>sixties</u> + 31 <u>ones</u>
(2 x <u>60</u>) + (31 x <u>1</u>) = 151

Match each of these to the correct Babylonian numerals.

257	a.	< VVV ⟨ ⟨ / VVV ⟨ ⟨
1000	b.	⟨ VV ⟨⟨ VVV / ⟨ ⟨⟨ VVV
1976	c.	VVVV < VVVV / VVV

3. For even larger numbers, additional powers of 60 were used as place values. Find the value of this Babylonian numeral.

$$\underbrace{\text{VV}} \quad \underbrace{⟨⟨ VVV} \quad \underbrace{⟨⟨}$$

$(2 \times 60^2) + (46 \times 60^1) + (40 \times 1) =$

$(2 \times 3600) + (46 \times 60) + (40 \times 1) =$ _____

1. The Babylonians used 60 as a denominator for fractions.

Study these examples	Then complete these.	
$1/2 = \dfrac{30}{60}$	$1/4 =$	$5/12 =$
$3/4 = \dfrac{45}{60}$	$3/10 =$	$7/20 =$
$2/5 = \dfrac{24}{60}$	$3/5 =$	$29/30 =$

2. In their cuneiform writing, only the numerators were given.
    Study the examples and complete the table.

numeral	$<$VVV	$\leqslant$V	$\leqslant\leqslant$ VVV VV	$\leqslant$VVV	$\leqslant\leqslant$ VV $<$ VV
value as a fraction	$\dfrac{13}{60}$	$\dfrac{21}{60}$			

3. Some fractions also used other powers of 60 as denominators.

Find the value for each numerator.	Simplify fractions before adding.	Express as a fraction and a decimal
$\leqslant\leqslant$ VV $<$ VVVV VVVV		
$\dfrac{42}{60^1} + \dfrac{18}{60^2}$ =	$\dfrac{42}{60} + \dfrac{18}{3600}$ =	$\dfrac{\quad}{200} = 0.\_\_\_$

4. Unfortunately, there was no way to tell where the fraction began in a
    Babylonian numeral. Find these three possible values for this numeral.

Babylonian numeral	Possible values
$\leqslant\leqslant$ VV $<$ VVVV VV VVVV	$(54 \times 60) + (18 \times 1) =$
	$(54 \times 1) + (18 \times 1/60) =$
	$(54 \times 1/60) + (18 \times 1/3600) =$

Here is a sketch of an ancient Babylonian tablet dating back to about 1700 BC. It shows three numerals written on the side and diagonal of a square. Let's see if you can unravel its secrets.

1. The number given for the side of the square is 30.

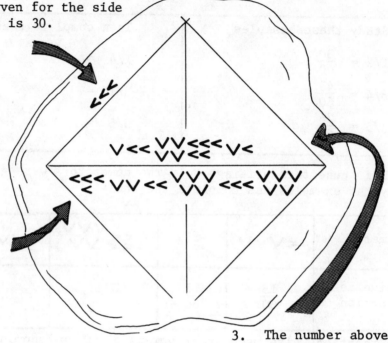

2. The number shown for the diagonal is:

$$42 + \frac{25}{60} + \frac{35}{3600}$$

3. The number above the diagonal is:

$$1 + \frac{24}{60} + \frac{51}{3600} + \frac{10}{216000}$$

Evaluate to six decimal places without rounding off.

42 = 42. <u>0</u> <u>0</u> <u>0</u> <u>0</u> <u>0</u> <u>0</u>	
$\frac{25}{60}$ = 0. _ _ _ _ _ _	
$\frac{35}{3600}$ = 0. _ _ _ _ _ _	
Sum 42. _ _ _ _ _ _	

Evaluate to six decimal places without rounding off.*

1 = 1. <u>0</u> <u>0</u> <u>0</u> <u>0</u> <u>0</u> <u>0</u>	
$\frac{24}{60}$ = 0. _ _ _ _ _ _	
$\frac{51}{3600}$ = 0. _ _ _ _ _ _	
$\frac{10}{216000}$ = 0. _ _ _ _ _ _	
Sum 1. _ _ _ _ _ _	

4. Find this product using 1.41421 as an approximation to $\sqrt{2}$. Compare the results with your answer to question 2.

$\sqrt{2}$ x 30 $\approx$ 1.41421 x 30

or _____

5. Mathematicians today know that the length of the diagonal of a square is $\sqrt{2}$ times the length of its side. Does it appear that the ancient Babylonians also knew this nearly 4000 years ago? _____

* Your answer should be a very good approximation to $\sqrt{2}$.

Additional Activities for
Computational Skills

Bolster, L. Carey. "Napier's Bones." Jan. 1973, 47–48. Students use a cutout set of Napier's bones to calculate products of whole numbers. (Grades 7–8)

Bolster, L. Carey. "Denominate Number Slide Rule." Jan. 1973, 49–50. Pupils use a cutout denominate number slide rule to find sums and differences of numbers of feet and inches. (Grades 7–8)

Allen, Charles E. "Mission—Calendar." May 1973, 435–38. Students complete a potpourri of calendar-related tasks including conducting a birthday survey of their class and recording and analyzing the data; representing sets using various methods; and using directed arrows to identify missing calendar numbers. (Grades 7–12)

Engelmeyer, William J. "Magic Squares." May 1975, 399–402. Students identify patterns within an 8 × 8 magic square and determine if 4 × 4 and 8 × 8 arrays of numbers are magic squares by computing "magic sums" and predicting "magic sums" with the use of a formula. (Grades 7–12)

Joshi, Vijay S. "Coded Events in American History." May 1976, 383–86. Pupils engage in a variety of bicentennial-related activities that reinforce computational skills. Activities include completing number tricks that result in the number 1976, using a code wheel to identify coded historical events, evaluating expressions written using the digits 1, 9, 7, and 6 in order, and writing expressions for the numbers 1–9 using the digits 1, 7, 7, and 6 in order. (Grades 7–9)

Kirschner, Michael M., and Thomas Liddy. "Two Bicentennial Puzzles." Oct. 1976, 479–82. Students complete a dot-to-dot puzzle and a crossnumber puzzle by converting to base ten numbers expressed in other bases or by carrying out calculations involving integers, fractions, and decimals. (Grades 7–9)

Oberle, William F. "Numbers and Mysticism." Oct. 1977, 599–602. Pupils determine whether given numbers are perfect, deficient, or abundant and whether given pairs of numbers are amicable by applying the appropriate definition. A number is assigned to each letter of the alphabet, and students use this assignment to determine whether names of persons or objects are associated with mystical numbers. Pairs of persons or objects are similarly compared. (Grades 7–12)

Activities for
Calculators

This section consists of four activities for use with hand-held calculators. The first activity, "Calculator Capers," provides students with an opportunity to discover generalizations about products of whole numbers by analyzing the patterns of numbers displayed by the calculator. The next activity, "Can You Predict the Repetend?" is designed so that pupils use calculators to complete tables and thereby discover patterns that permit prediction of the repetend when a whole number is divided by 9, 99, 999, and so forth.

One valuable use of calculators in the mathematics classroom is in the area of applications. One such example is the activity "Compound Interest à la Simple Calculator." Here pupils explore the relationship between simple interest and compound interest by using calculators to develop inductively the compound-interest formula. "Calculator Crossword Puzzle" illustrates how calculators can be used to reinforce learning in an entertaining fashion. In this activity, students are to use their knowledge of rules for the order of operations and their calculators to evaluate given mathematical expressions and then invert the calculator to read words that are used to complete a crossword puzzle.

The activity "Pattern Gazing" in the Problem Solving section illustrates nicely how a calculator can be used to facilitate problem solving. Calculators could similarly be used for the last portion of the activity "Probability and Pi" in the same section.

For additional calculator activities consult the annotated listing at the end of this section and recent issues of the *Mathematics Teacher*.

CALCULATOR CAPERS

*By Rosemary Schmalz, S.P., Saint Mary-of-the-Woods College
Saint Mary-of-the-Woods, IN 47876*

Teacher's Guide

Grade level: 7–11

Materials: Calculators and one set of worksheets for each student

Objective: To provide an opportunity for students to discover numerical patterns

Procedure: Sheets 1, 2, and 3 are independent of each other and can therefore be used on separate days. If there are only a limited number of hand-held calculators available you may wish to have students work on this activity in small groups. Provide each student with a copy of one or more of the worksheets. Be sure pupils understand the directions before they begin.

Supplementary activities: Students can be challenged to demonstrate why these patterns occur. They might also be encouraged to find other numerical patterns. To get them started you might have them investigate the pattern formed by the following products: 4×9, 44×99, 444×999, and so on. Other patterns can then be generated by replacing the 4 with a different single-digit number. A variety of additional patterns may be found in Carman and Carman (1970).

REFERENCE

Carman, R., and M. Carman. "Number Patterns." *Arithmetic Teacher* 17 (Dec. 1970): 637–39.

Editorial comment: This activity illustrates how calculators can be used to discover generalizations about products of whole numbers by studying patterns that are displayed. In this setting even the pupil weak in computational skills has opportunities to experience the enjoyment of creative activity. Calculators could similarly be used to study patterns involving fractions handled as quotients of whole numbers. Pupils could find the decimal equivalent of such fractions as 1/3, 1/33, and 1/333 and then predict that for 1/33333. By considering the pattern of decimal equivalents of a sequence of fractions such as 1/2, 2/3, 3/4, 4/5, 5/6, . . . , students can develop an intuitive understanding of limits. As another variation, your students might enjoy using patterns to find a winning strategy for the following two-person calculator game. One player chooses a target number between 30 and 60. Players then take turns entering and "adding on" a nonzero single digit number until one player hits the target. The pupil who reaches the target wins. This game could be modified to use subtraction, multiplication, or division. An important by-product of pattern-finding activities with calculators might be an increased interest on the part of students in the study of number ideas.

Calculator Capers

For each part, do the problems in the first column with a calculator. Then, by looking for patterns in the results, predict the answers to the problems in the second column without actually calculating them.

A.

(1 x 9) + 2 = _____   (12,345 x 9) + 6 = _____

(12 x 9) + 3 = _____   (1,234,567 x 9) + 8 = _____

(123 x 9) + 4 = _____   (_____ x 9) + __ = 111,111,111

B.

(9 x 9) + 7 = _____   (9,876 x 9) + 4 = _____

(98 x 9) + 6 = _____   (9,876,543 x 9) + 1 = _____

(987 x 9) + 5 = _____   (_____ x 9) + __ = 888,888

C.

(1 x 9) − 1 = _____   (4,321 x 9) − 1 = _____

(21 x 9) − 1 = _____   (7,654,321 x 9) − 1 = _____

(321 x 9) − 1 = _____   (_____ x 9) − 1 = 5,888,888

D.

(1 x 8) + 1 = _____   (1,234 x 8) + 4 = _____

(12 x 8) + 2 = _____   (12,345,678 x 8) + 8 = _____

(123 x 8) + 3 = _____   (_____ x 8) + __ = 987,654

E.

(99 x 1) + 1 = _____   (99 x 5) + 5 = _____

(99 x 2) + 2 = _____   (99 x 8) + 8 = _____

(99 x 3) + 3 = _____   (99 x __) + __ = 700

Calculator Capers

For each part, do the problems in the first column with a calculator. Then, by looking for patterns in the results, predict the answers to the problems in the second column without actually calculating them.

F.

99 x 9 = _____   99 x 5 = _____

99 x 8 = _____   99 x 2 = _____

99 x 7 = _____   99 x __ = 396

G.

37 x 3 = _____   37 x 15 = _____

37 x 6 = _____   37 x 24 = _____

37 x 9 = _____   37 x __ = 666

H.

999,999 x 2 = _____   999,999 x 6 = _____

999,999 x 3 = _____   999,999 x 9 = _____

999,999 x 8 = _____   999,999 x __ = 6,999,993

I.

15,873 x 7 = _____   15,873 x 35 = _____

15,873 x 14 = _____   15,873 x 56 = _____

15,873 x 21 = _____   15,873 x __ = 777,777

J.

3,367 x 3 = _____   3,367 x 15 = _____

3,367 x 6 = _____   3,367 x 21 = _____

3,367 x 9 = _____   3,367 x __ = 80,808

Calculator Capers

For each part, do the problems in the first column with a calculator. Then, by looking for patterns in the results, predict the answers to the problems in the second column without actually calculating them.

K.

$(11)^2 = $ _____

$(111)^2 = $ _____

$(1,111)^2 = $ _____

$(11,111)^2 = $ _____

$(11,111,111)^2 = $ _____

$($ _____ $)^2 = 12,345,654,321$

L.

$(34)^2 = $ _____

$(334)^2 = $ _____

$(3,334)^2 = $ _____

$(33,334)^2 = $ _____

$(33,333,334)^2 = $ _____

$($ _____ $)^2 = 111,111,555,556$

M.

$(67)^2 = $ _____

$(667)^2 = $ _____

$(6,667)^2 = $ _____

$(66,667)^2 = $ _____

$(6,666,667)^2 = $ _____

$($ _____ $)^2 = 4,444,444,488,888,889$

N.

$(98)^2 = $ _____

$(998)^2 = $ _____

$(9,998)^2 = $ _____

$(99,998)^2 = $ _____

$(99,999,998)^2 = $ _____

$($ _____ $)^2 = 999,996,000,004$

O.

$(49)^2 = $ _____

$(499)^2 = $ _____

$(4,999)^2 = $ _____

$(49,999)^2 = $ _____

$(4,999,999)^2 = $ _____

$($ _____ $)^2 = 24,999,990,000,001$

CAN YOU PREDICT THE REPETEND?

December 1976

By Douglas Woodburn, Perry Hall Junior High School, Baltimore County, Maryland

Teacher's Guide

Grade level: 7–12
Materials: Calculator; activity sheets for each student
Objective: Students will use a calculator to discover patterns that will allow them to predict the repetend when a number is divided by 9, 99, and 999.

Discussion: This activity should not be attempted unless students have access to a hand calculator or a table-top model. For many students, the term *repetend* may be new. Be sure they understand that the repetend is the repeating digit or series of digits in a repeating decimal.

The general pattern for predicting the repetend is this:

1. The number of 9s in the divisor is the number of digits in the repetend. If dividing by 9, the repetend will be one digit; by 99, two digits; by 999, three digits; and so on.

2. Dividing by 9
   Separate the digits and add. If the sum has more digits than the repetend, add the digits in the sum.

   $5885 \div 9$
   $5 + 8 + 8 + 5 = 26$
   $2 + 6 = 8$
   The repetend is 8.

3. Dividing by 99
   Group digits in pairs from right to left. Then use the same process as when dividing by 9.

   $2689 \div 99$
   $26 + 89 = 115$
   $1 + 15 = 16$
   The repetend is 16.

4. Dividing by 999
   Group digits in threes from right to left, and use the same process.

   $13562 \div 999$
   $13 + 562 = 575$
   The repetend is 575.

These patterns should develop as the students work through sheets one, two, and three. It is suggested that the teacher do the activities prior to using them with students in order to anticipate students' questions.

You may wish to extend the activity by finding the pattern when dividing by 11.

Editorial comment: Students who finish this activity more quickly than others might be challenged to discover a technique for finding the whole number remainder when division of whole numbers is done with a calculator. This should reinforce their understanding of the division algorithm. This technique could then be generalized to find the decimal expansion of a number such as 1/17.

Can You Predict the Repetend?

Divide by 9.

The repetend is the repeating digit or series of digits in a repeating decimal. $123 \div 9 = 13.66\overline{6}$. The repetend is <u>6</u>. $728 \div 99 = 7.3\overline{35}$. The repetend is <u>35</u>. In this activity, you will be observing patterns and developing rules for <u>predicting</u> the repetend.

1. Use a calculator for all divisions. Complete the chart.

DIVIDEND Divide by 9	4	6	3	2	1	7	8	5
REPETEND	4							

2. Write the pattern you observe for dividing a single digit by 9.

_____

3. Find the repetend for these numbers:

DIVIDEND Divide by 9	12	16	32	43	25	60	71	115	204	143
REPETEND										

4. Write the pattern for finding the repetend. (HINT: Look at the sum of the digits in the dividend.)

_____

5. Find the repetend.

DIVIDEND Divide by 9	58	86	38	46	98	139	433	168	5613	48167
REPETEND										

Look at your results in problem 5. Since the divisor (9) has only one digit, the repetend will have only one digit. Find the sum of the digits in the dividend, and then add the digits in the sum until the sum is a single digit.

6. Use the rule stated above to predict the repetend. Then check your predictions with the calculator.

DIVIDEND Divide by 9	73	435	6245	35265	42356	88888	52736	982645
PREDICTED REPETEND								
REPETEND								

Can You Predict the Repetend?

Divide by 99.

You developed a rule for predicting repetends when dividing by 9.
See if it applies to division by 99.

1. Complete the chart. Use a calculator.

DIVIDEND Divide by 99 REPETEND	6	8	23	46	89	64	73	37	49	87	44	88

2. What pattern do you observe? _____

3. Find the repetend.

DIVIDEND Divide by 99 REPETEND	125	421	142	283	450	804	716	826	489

4. Write the pattern for finding the repetend. (HINT: Separate 125
    into 1 and 25.) _____

5. Since the divisor 99 has only two digits, the repetend will have
    only two digits. Predict the repetend, then check with the cal-
    culator.

DIVIDEND Divide by 99	5	23	246	745	289	587	868	598	2315	8549	76834
PREDICTED REPETEND											
REPETEND											

Can You Predict the Repetend?

Divide by 999.

1. Complete the chart.

DIVIDEND Divide by 999 REPETEND	3	8	25	63	89	462	123	809	900

A pattern seems obvious, but let's try some larger numbers.

2. Complete the charts.

DIVIDEND Divide by 999 REPETEND	1402	3512	4132	5627	4839	8786	8569	7348

DIVIDEND Divide by 999 REPETEND	31124	25631	79876	85697	401132	23167	112678

3. Describe the pattern for finding the repetend when a number is divided by 999.

_____

BONUS:

4. A rule does exist for predicting repetends when dividing any number by any member of the set 9, 99, 999, 9999, and so forth. Try to develop it.

COMPOUND INTEREST
A LA SIMPLE CALCULATOR

May 1979

By William D. Jamski, Indiana University Southeast, New Albany, IN 47150

Teacher's Guide

Grade Level: 8–12

Materials: Student worksheets, one set of classroom transparencies, and at least one calculator for every two students

Objectives: Students will explore the relationship between simple interest and compound interest by using calculators to develop inductively and intuitively the relationship

$$A = p\left(1 + \frac{r}{n}\right)^n.$$

Procedure: Before attempting this activity, students should be able to operate a four-function hand calculator. Each should be familiar with percent, the simple interest formula ($I = prt$), and the terms interest, principal, rate, period, and amount. After these prerequisite skills have been presented, sheet 1 should be distributed to check mastery. The notions of annually, semiannually, and quarterly are also developed here. After students have successfully finished sheet 1, sheet 2 can be distributed and completed under close teacher supervision. The second activity develops the compound interest concept. The effect of compounding is also graphically explored. With each activity appropriate calculator use should be encouraged. Sheet 3 presents several problems for determining the de-

gree to which pertinent concepts have been learned.

Answers

Sheet 1: 1(d) 0.05, 0.025, 0.0125; 1(e) 0.0525, 0.02625, 0.013125; 1(f) 0.055, 0.0275, 0.01375; 1(g) 0.0575, 0.02875, 0.014375; 1(h) 0.06, 0.03, 0.015; 1(i) 0.0625, 0.03125, 0.015625; 1(j) 0.065, 0.0325, 0.01625; 2(a) 56.25; 2(b) 24.43; 2(c) 16.70; 2(d) 500; 2(e) 4½; 2(f) 180. *Sheet 2:* 115.76, 5.78(8), 121.54(8), $1.05^4 \times 100$; 121.54, 6.07(7), 127.61(7), $1.05^5 \times 100$; 127.61, 6.38(05), 133.99(05), $1.05^6 \times 100$; 133.99, 6.69(95), 140.68(95), $1.05^7 \times 100$; 140.68, 7.03(4), 147.7(14), $1.05^8 \times 100$. Each period's interest is added to the next period's principal. Not taking into consideration that the amounts of money were rounded down to the nearest penny,

$$A = p\left(1 + \frac{r}{n}\right)^n.$$

The graph for simple interest appears straight and crosses 200 at 10 years, while the graph of compound interest curves and crosses 200 at 7½ years. *Sheet 3:* (1) $862.50, (2) 6½%, (3) $23.75 in interest is earned both ways. Over only one interest period, interest cannot be earned on interest. (4) $5.93 + $6.00 + $6.07 + $6.15 = $24.15, $24.15 − $23.75 = 40¢, (5) 6.13%, $(1.015)^4 = 1.0613(6)$, (6) 44 periods (11 years).

Editorial comment: This activity provides a nice setting to illustrate an application of the automatic constant capability of many calculators. Suppose you deposit $1000 in an account that is compounded semiannually at a rate of 12 percent and you wish to determine the amount of funds available after two years. If your calculator uses the first factor as an automatic constant for multiplication, you can obtain the answer by simply pressing 1.06 × 1000 = = = =.

Students may want to explore with their calculators the effect on interest earned over a fixed period of time as the number of compoundings increases. For example, find the interest earned on $100 at 6 percent per year compounded annually, semiannually, quarterly, monthly, weekly, and daily. Institutions advertising "continuous" compounding really mean "daily" compounding. However, were the number of conversions to increase without bound, the interest earned would continue to increase but not without bound.

REVIEW OF BASIC CONCEPTS

Complete the following activities, using the calculator provided as needed. Scratch work may be done in the available space. Be sure to have questions answered before trying to go further.

1. Complete the following chart.

	Annual Rate	Equivalent Decimal	Semiannual Rate	Quarterly Rate
(a)	4 %	0.04	0.02	0.01
(b)	$4\frac{1}{2}$%	0.045	0.0225	0.01125
(c)	4 3/4%	0.0475	0.02375	0.011875
(d)	5%			
(e)	$5\frac{1}{4}$%			
(f)	$5\frac{1}{2}$%			
(g)	5 3/4%			
(h)	6%			
(i)	$6\frac{1}{4}$%			
(j)	$6\frac{1}{2}$%			

2. Taking into account the simple interest formula, I = prt (where I is the amount of interest, p is the principal, r is the annual rate, and t is the number of years or fractional part of a year), find each of the missing values. Where appropriate, consider 360 days as a business year. All dollar amounts are rounded down to the nearest cent.

	Interest	Principal	Annual Rate	Time
(a)	$_____	$375.00	5 %	3 years
(b)	$_____	$850.00	5 3/4%	6 months
(c)	$_____	$495.00	$4\frac{1}{2}$%	270 days
(d)	$150.00	$_____	6 %	5 years
(e)	$45.00	$1500.00	___%	8 months
(f)	$37.50	$1200.00	$6\frac{1}{4}$%	_____ days

COMPOUNDING

1. Determine what happens to $100 compounded semiannually at 10% over
   4 years. Round down to the nearest cent.

Principal	Semiannual Rate	Interest	Amount		
$100.00	½(10%)	$5.00	$105.00		$1.05^1 \times 100$
$105.00	0.05	$5.25	$110.25	end of year 1	$1.05^2 \times 100$
$110.25	0.05	$5.51(25)	$115.76(25)		$1.05^3 \times 100$
_____	0.05	_____	_____	end of year 2	$1.05^4 \times 100$
_____	0.05	_____	_____		_____
_____	0.05	_____	_____	end of year 3	_____
_____	0.05	_____	_____		_____
_____	0.05	_____	_____	end of year 4	_____

   Describe two methods by which you can determine the amount of money
   available at the end of 5 years.

2. Using ●'s, graph what happens to $100 invested at 10% simple interest
   over a period of 10 years. Using x's, graph what happens to $100
   compounded semiannually at 10% interest per year over a period of
   10 years. Use your answers to exercise 1 above. Discuss the results.

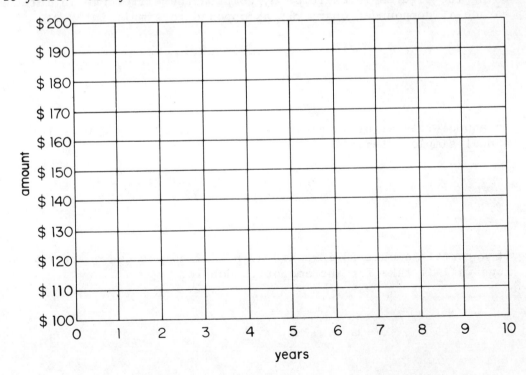

RELATED PROBLEMS

Using the results from sheets 1 and 2 and your calculator, as needed, solve the following problems.

1. Compute the simple interest earned on a principal of $3750 invested at 5 3/4% annually for a period of 4 years.

2. Compute the annual rate of interest needed to generate $19.50 in simple interest over a 3-year period on a principal of $100.00.

3. $500 is invested at 4 3/4% annually for 1 year. Compare the results of simple interest and compounding annually. Explain the results.

4. Using the figures in exercise 3, compare the difference in interest earned if compounded quarterly as opposed to simple interest.

5. An annual rate of 6% when compounded quarterly yields what rate of annual simple interest?

6. If a certain amount is invested at 6 1/2% compounded quarterly, how long will it take for the amount to double?

CALCULATOR CROSSWORD PUZZLE

By Joseph F. Goodhue, Newport High School, Newport, NH 03773

Teacher's Guide

Grade Level: 7–12

Materials: Eight-place pocket calculator (preferably with a memory)

Objectives: In this activity students use pocket calculators to demonstrate their knowledge of the correct order of operations for a given mathematical expression.

Directions: The first worksheet provides some warmup exercises that review the rules for the order of operations and establishes the procedure for spelling out words by inverting the calculator. In general, multiplication and division take priority over addition and subtraction unless symbols of grouping (parentheses, brackets, and braces) are involved. The rule for the order of operations is as follows:

First carry out all operations within symbols of grouping. Then perform multiplications and divisions in the order in which they occur from left to right. Finally, perform all additions and subtractions.

For each entry in the crossword puzzle (sheet 2), the student performs the indicated computation, gets a result, and then inverts the calculator to read a word or abbreviation. The word or abbreviation is checked against the verbal cue and then entered into the appropriate cells in the crossword puzzle diagram.

Looking at 1 Across on the crossword puzzle (sheet 2), we need a four-letter word for "legendary Viking." Entering the expression $5(200 \times 15 - 10 \times 172 - 6)$ on the calculator in the correct order of operation should produce the number

$$6370.$$

Inverting the calculator, we read the name

$$OLE9,$$

which we write in the given spaces in our puzzle.

The answer sheet (sheet 3) can be reproduced for the students if desired.

REFERENCE

Vannatta, Glen D., A. Wilson Goodwin, and Harold P. Fawcett. *Algebra Two: A Modern Course.* Columbus, Ohio: Charles E. Merrill, 1966.

Editorial comment: Many calculators will drop the last zero in a decimal computation such as that required for 25 DOWN. In this case, the three digits behind the decimal point in the answer provide the last three letters of the required word. As a related activity you might give pupils a word such as *SLEIgh* and ask them to find a numerical expression whose inverted answer is the word.

1. In each of the following, use a calculator and the rule for the
    order of operations to compute the given expression. When you get
    an answer, turn your calculator upside down and read the word.
    Record intermediate steps and the word.

    Example: 123(45 + 72) - 40584 ÷ 6 + 13 x 7

             = 123 x 117 - 40584 ÷ 6 + 13 x 7

             = 14391 - 6764 + 91

             = 7718

               B I L L
               _ _ _ _

a)   (10+13(236+587)-595x5)÷10 000   b)   37+(20+(19+13x41-5))

c)   96(78-24÷8-25)+24x25-91   d)   623x411-213x303+1296÷4x579-288-16

2. Write the letters that correspond to the numerals:

    0   1   2   3   4   5   6   7   8   9

    _   _   _   _   _   _   _   _   _   _

3. Make your calculator read these words:

                    Keys to Press

    SIZE   _____

    gIggLE   _____

    hOBBLE   _____

    BOBSLED   _____

ACROSS

1. Legendary Viking
   5(200x15-10x172-6)

4. East African river
   5(115889x3+2)

9. Actor Hope
   (12x199+36)÷3

11. African desert
    (350x20+40x5)÷4+6

12. Rumanian river
    15(4x895+3x3)

13. Siberian river
    (14x20x5+40)÷(5x3+3)

15. Actor Greene (initials)
    2x15-5x2+5x8+7

18. _____ Horizonte
    0.8856÷12

20. Swiss lake
    2(9x7x58+5)

22. Filmmaker Goldwyn (initials)
    (38x14+11x4)÷8-8+1

24. Actor Bridges
    (16.6-6.2)÷(5x30-20)

27. Belgian river
    25x20(35x2+1)+37

28. Dutch painter
    8x25(4x5+3)+6

31. State
    (50(7x4+5))÷3+221

32. Nigerian Mountain Range
    15(300x320+1223)

33. Make dirty
    5x27(9x7-10)-50

DOWN

1. French river
   10((70x10)÷2+1)

2. _____ of Reims
   4x0.0220+0.0003

3. Nazi minister (WW II)
   88888888-31500888+150x2+6

5. German sculptor
   (313254+305505+5x29)÷8

6. Actor Bridges
   0.80÷16+0.03

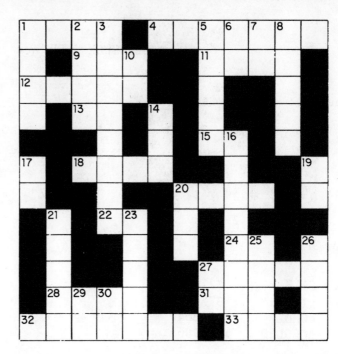

7. Hitler's mistress (initials)
   8x7+9x3

8. Belgian University
   36007+15.5x20

10. College Degree
    (350+32x0.3)÷6.2

14. Self   0.08x0.9-0.009

16. Same as 3 Down

17. Old Saxon (abbr.)
    (9x39-1)÷7

19. Old Latin (abbr.)
    3(8x21-4)÷6+1-13

20. Little _____ Horn
    22x32-16x6+10

21. Capt. of H.M.S. *Bounty*
    2((14x12+3)x(15x9)+4)

23. Belonging to 28 Across
    6(2733÷3x10-9)÷10000

25. Norwegian city
    0.1230-0.0340-0.0140

26. Telephone inventor
    15+8x8x11x11-21

27. Long Island (abbr.)
    (21x14-5)÷17

29. Old English (abbr.)
    (645÷15+47)÷3

30. Mathematician Boole (initials)
    (12x79-2)÷(30÷6+6)

Sheet 1:

1. a) 0.7734   hELLO   b) 604   hOg

    c) 5309   GOES   d) 378806   gOBBLE

2. 0   1   2   3   4   5   6   7   8   9

    O   I   Z   E   h   S   g   L   B   G

    or D

3. SIZE   3215
    gIggLE   376616
    hOBBLE   378804
    BOBSLED   .0375808

Sheet 2:

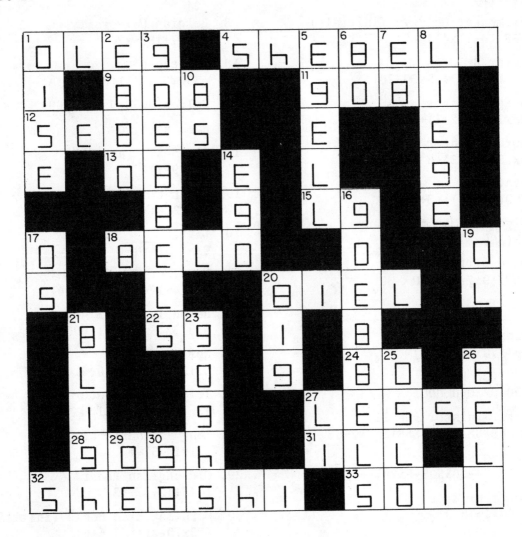

Additional Activities for
Calculators

Smith, Susan. "Calculating Order." Sept. 1978, 519–22, 530. Calculators are used to evaluate arithmetical expressions designed to develop and reinforce students' concept of order of operations. Pupils also rewrite expressions to obtain equivalent expressions that permit the numbers and operations to be entered in the calculator in order from left to right. (Grades 7–10)

Miller, William A., and Donald W. Hazekamp. "Calculator Graphing." Dec. 1978, 759–62. Students use calculators to complete tables for the relations $y = x^2$, $y = 1/x$, and $x^2 + y^2 = 1$. Ordered pairs are then plotted on a prepared coordinate system and the corresponding curves are sketched. (Grades 7–12)

Bone, Dorothea D. "Sine and Cosine Functions with a Calculator." Oct. 1980, 521–24, 529. Pupils use calculators to complete a table of values for the sine and cosine functions and use the table to discover properties of these functions and to draw their graphs. (Grades 9–12)

Olsen, Melfried. "It's a Factor of Life." Dec. 1980, 681–84. Working in small groups to which are assigned specific subsets of the numbers 1–100, students use calculators to determine the number of positive factors of each number in their assigned set. Group results are entered in a prepared table that is subsequently analyzed by the class for patterns. (Grades 7–9)

Activities for
Geometry

Many topics in geometry lend themselves to creative mathematical involvement on the part of the learner. The first activity, "Graphs and Games," explores topological properties of the plane. Students discover and apply Euler's formula regarding connected planar graphs and then play and and analyze the game of Sprouts.

The activity "Getting the Point!" provides a creative introduction to the coordinate plane. In this activity pupils plot points on a rectangular coordinate system and connect them to produce pictures. The production of art is also the focus of the "Designs with Tessellations" activity. Students complete designs created from tessellations of triangles and quadrilaterals on a square grid and then create an Escher type of tessellation based on an equilateral triangle.

The next two activities focus on the Pythagorean theorem. In "Preparing for Pythagoras" pupils use prepared triangular and square dot paper to discover the relationship among the areas of similar figures constructed on the sides of right triangles. "Pythagorean Puzzles" provides students with three dissection puzzles which, when completed, demonstrate the Pythagorean relationship.

"Polyhedra from Cardboard and Elastics" provides students patterns for the faces and directions for using rubber bands to assemble sturdy models of the five Platonic solids and a rhombicosidodecahedron. The next activity, "Poinsot Stars," investigates the mathematics behind curve stitching. Pupils discover the number of Poinsot stars and the number of regular Poinsot stars determined by n equally spaced points on a circle.

In the final activity, "Curves from Straight Lines and Circles," students draw a family of parabolas on a worksheet consisting of concentric circles and parallel lines by marking the points of intersection of numbered lines and circles. Families of ellipses and hyperbolas are drawn on worksheets consisting of pairs of concentric circles by marking the points of intersection of numbered circles whose sum or difference is a given constant.

Many additional geometry activities are listed and briefly described at the end of this section.

GRAPHS AND GAMES

February 1975

By Christian R. Hirsch, Western Michigan University
Kalamazoo, Michigan

Teacher's Guide

Grade level: 7–10

Materials: One set of worksheets for each student and a set of transparencies for class discussion

Objectives: The student will (1) discover and apply Euler's formula regarding connected planar graphs and (2) play and analyze the game of Sprouts.

Directions: Distribute the worksheets to each student.

Sheet 1. Students should have little difficulty discovering the formula, $V + R = E + 2$. Point out that the edges of a graph need not be straight and that they may intersect only at the vertices. Students might investigate whether an analogous formula holds for vertices, faces, and edges of polyhedra.

Sheet 2. In this activity students discover that a graph is traversable if it has exactly 0 or 2 odd vertices. In the first case the starting vertex can be chosen arbitrarily, whereas in the second case the starting and finishing vertices must be the two odd vertices.

Sheet 3. Where necessary, show students how a graph can be formed for exercise

8a by letting the four pieces of land be vertices. Exercise 8c is the famous problem of the seven bridges of Königsberg. See Newman (1956) for a brief historical account. For an analysis of the game of Sprouts, described in exercise 9, see Gardner (1967). You may want to organize a Sprouts tournament for the class and then use the graphs generated to reinforce earlier discoveries about graphs. Variations of the game can be made by starting with 2, 4, or more dots. Interesting inquiries include the following: Must there always be a winner? Is the outcome determined by who starts? What are the minimum and maximum number of moves possible?

REFERENCES

Gardner, Martin. "Mathematical Games." *Scientific American* 217 (July 1967): 112–15.

Laible, Jon M. "Try Graph Theory for a Change." MATHEMATICS TEACHER 63 (November 1970): 557–62.

Meyer, Walter. "Garbage Collection, Sunday Strolls, and Soldering Problems." MATHEMATICS TEACHER 65 (April 1972): 307–9.

Newman, James Roy, ed. *The World of Mathematics.* Vol. 1. New York: Simon & Schuster, 1956.

Ore, Oystein. *Graphs and Their Uses.* New York: Random House, 1963.

Editorial comment: The polyhedral analogue of Euler's formula for sheet 1 is investigated in the activity "Painting Polyhedra" listed at the end of this section. Students might find it helpful to place a sheet of tracing paper over each graph when checking traversability on sheet 2. With respect to the game of Sprouts, it can be shown that the minimum number of moves in an *n*-dot game will be $2n$, whereas the maximum number will be $3n - 1$.

Figures of the sort shown below are called <u>graphs</u>. Each point indicated by a heavy dot is called a <u>vertex</u>, and each arc connecting two vertices is called an <u>edge</u>. Each separated part of the plane formed by the graph is called a <u>region</u>. Note that graph (a) separates the plane into 2 regions, the region inside the graph and the region outside the graph.

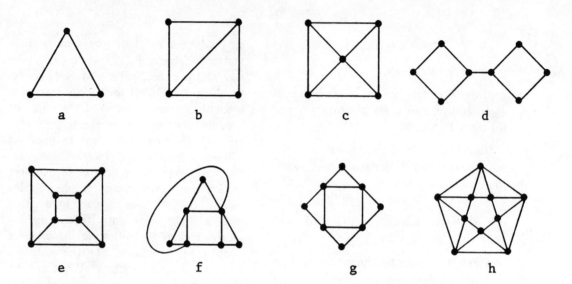

1. Complete the table below.

Graph	Edges (E)	Vertices (V)	Regions (R)	V + R
a	3	3	2	5
b				
c				
d				
e				
f				
g				
h				

2. Write down a formula relating the numbers V, R, and E.

3. Draw another graph of your own and count V, R, and E.
   Does your formula also work for this graph?

4. How many regions would be formed by a graph with 5 vertices and 12 edges?
   Draw one such graph to verify your answer.

5. A graph is said to be <u>traversable</u> if it can be traced in one sweep without lifting the pencil from the paper and without tracing the same edge more than once. Vertices may be passed through more than once.

   Determine which of the graphs on Sheet 1 are traversable. For those that are, mark the vertex where you start (S) and the vertex where you finish (F).

6. A vertex is said to be <u>even</u> if there is an even number of edges leading from it.

   A vertex is said to be <u>odd</u> if there is an odd number of edges leading from it.

   Complete the table below for the graphs on Sheet 1.

Graph	Number of Even Vertices	Number of Odd Vertices	Traversable
a	3	0	Yes
b			
c			
d			
e			
f			
g			
h			

7. a. Can you traverse a graph if all the vertices are even?

   b. Can you traverse a graph if it has two odd vertices?

   c. Can you traverse a graph if it has more than two odd vertices?

   d. If a graph is traversable, does it matter at which vertex you start or at which vertex you finish?

Activities from the *Mathematics Teacher* 53

8. a. The city of Kaliningrad is located on the banks and on two islands of the Pregel River. The various parts of the city are connected by 9 bridges (one a railroad bridge) as shown in the figure below. Is it possible to make a walking tour of the city that crosses each of the bridges exactly once?

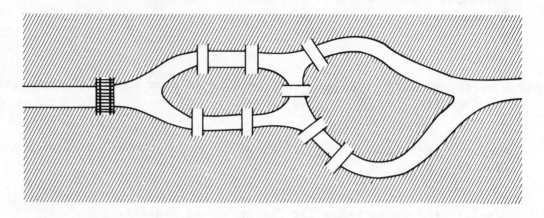

   b. Could such a tour be taken if the railroad bridge is excluded?

   c. Could this be done if the railroad bridge <u>and</u> a bridge on the lower right side are excluded?

9. Below is an interesting game involving graphs, which you can play with a friend.

   a. Mark 3 dots on a sheet of paper.
   b. Take turns drawing arcs according to these rules:

   1. Each arc must join 2 dots or a dot to itself.
   2. No arc may be crossed, and no dot may be the endpoint of more than 3 arcs.
   3. When an arc is drawn, the player must mark a new dot somewhere on it.

   c. The winner is the last player to draw a "legal" arc.

EXAMPLE

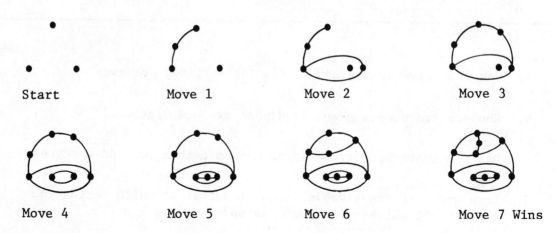

| Start | Move 1 | Move 2 | Move 3 |
| Move 4 | Move 5 | Move 6 | Move 7 Wins |

GETTING THE POINT!

November 1977

By Marcia F. Snyder, Menlo Park, CA 94025

Teacher's Guide

Grade level: 7–12

Materials: Worksheet with the listing of points to plot. Graph sheets 1 and 2 with axes drawn. Ruler.

Objectives: Just plotting random points can be boring. These two activities, however, with the promise of turning out dot-to-dot pictures, will generate enthusiasm for learning how to plot points properly.

Graph 1 is a good initial experience in familiarizing students with the rectangular coordinate system by locating points in the first quadrant only.

Graph 2 provides more practice in plotting and emphasizes all four quadrants.

Activity Outcome: Once students have mastered the art of point plotting, why not encourage them to create their own dot-to-dot designs? Give them extra credit for their efforts, and allow other students to work them out, too.

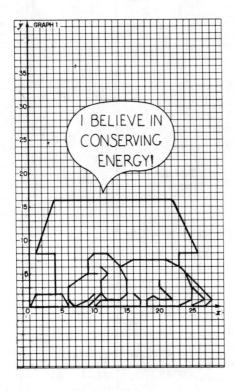

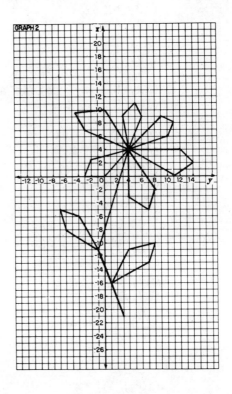

Editorial comment: The motivational aspects of this activity make it useful not only for the study of coordinate graphing but also for the review and maintenance of the skill at other times. An interesting modification of this activity can be made by reversing the process. You draw a figure on the coordinate grid and have your students find the corresponding set of coordinates sequenced properly from a given starting point. This can be effectively used as an oral review by asking each successive student in your class for the coordinates of the next point used in the figure.

WORKSHEET: GRAPHING PICTURES

Plot the following points, connecting them one by one. When you finish, you should have a picture.

GRAPH 1

Start at (4, 2)   Begin
     (5, 2)   again at (20, 4)
     (6, 0)   (20, 3)
     (0, 0)   (22, 1)
     (1, 2)   (20, 1)
     (4, 2)   (19, 1½)
     (4, 8)   (18, 1)
     (1, 8)   (18, 0)
     (4, 16)   (23, 0)
     (22, 16)   (25, 1)
     (26, 8)   (25, 3)
     (23, 8)   (24, 5)
     (23, 6)   (23, 6) Break
     (21, 7)
     (16, 7)
     (14, 6)   Begin
     (12, 8)   again at (24, 5)
     (10, 8)   (28, 1)
     (9, 7)   (27, 0)
     (9, 5)   (25, 0)
     (6, 3)   (27, 1)
     (6, 1)   (25, 3) Break
     (7, 0)
     (9, 0)
     (11, 2)   Begin
     (12, 1)   again at (11, 6)
     (11, 1)   (12, 5)
     (10, 0)   (11, 4)
     (17, 0)   (11, 2)
     (17, 1)   (12, 1)
     (16, 2) Break   (14, 1)
                 (15, 2)
Begin   (15, 4)
again at (9, 5)   (14, 6) Break
     (10½, 5) Break
              Begin
              again at (7, 0)
                 (9, 1)
                 (10, 2) Stop

GRAPH 2

Begin at (4, 4)
     (0, 0)
     (-3, 0)
     (-2, 2½)
     (4, 4)
     (-3, 7)
     (-3½, 9½)
     (0, 10)
     (4, 4)
     (3, 9)
     (5, 11)
     (6, 9)
     (4, 4)
     (9, 9)
     (11, 8)
     (10, 6)
     (4, 4)
     (12, 4)
     (14, 2)
     (11, 0)
     (4, 4)
     (8, -2)
     (7, -5)
     (4, -3)
     (4, 4)
     (-1, -11)
     (-4, -6)
     (-7, -5)
     (-6, -8)
     (-1, -11)
     (3, -21) Break

Begin
again at (1, -16)
     (4, -11)
     (8, -10)
     (7, -13)
     (1, -16) Stop

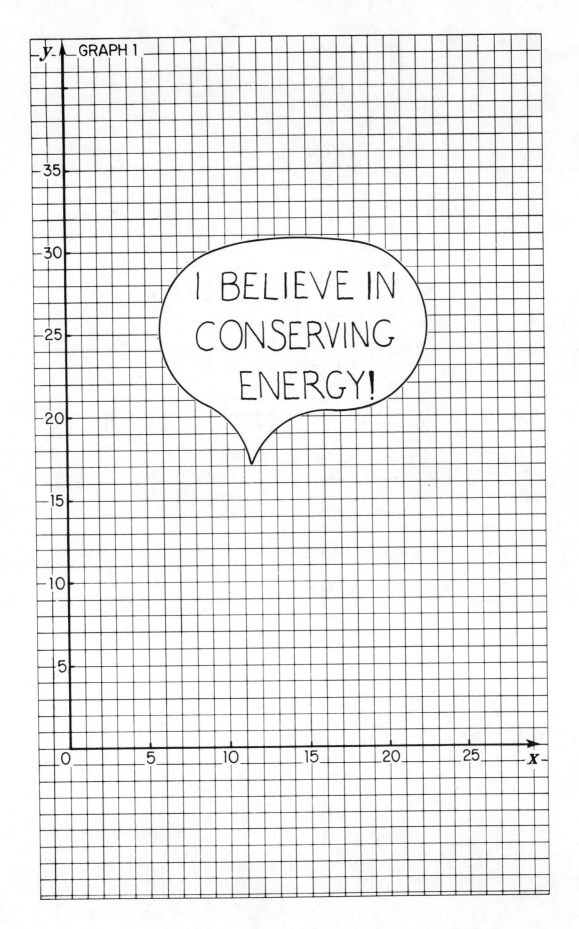

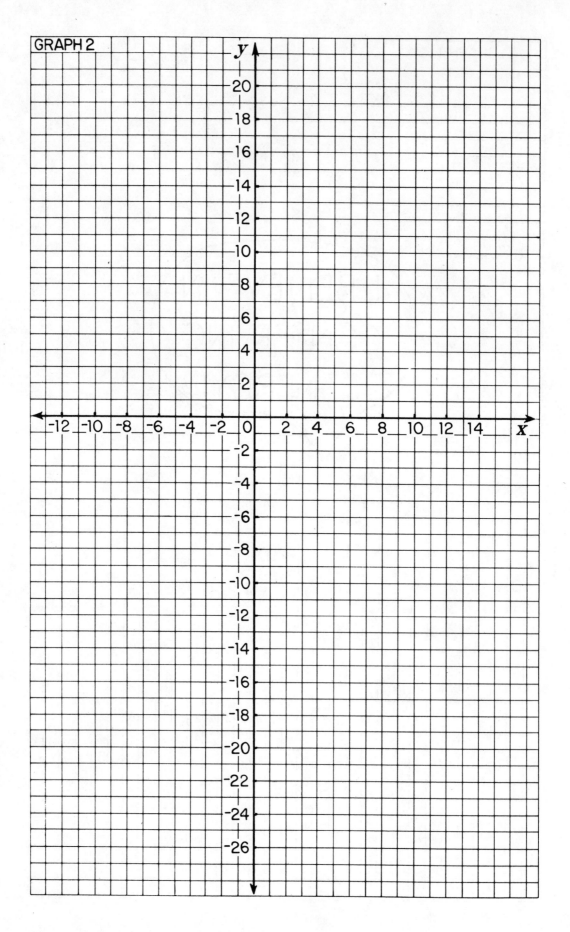

GRAPH 2

DESIGNS WITH TESSELLATIONS

By Evan M. Maletsky, Montclair State College, Upper Montclair, NJ 07043

Teacher's Guide

Grade level: **7–12**

Materials: One set of worksheets and a ruler for each student. A set of transparencies for classroom demonstration and discussion. Several sets of congruent triangles and quadrilaterals.

Objectives: To develop skill in drawing congruent polygons on a rectangular grid. To construct tessellations from various polygons. To show how designs can be created from basic tessellation patterns.

Directions: First show how congruent triangles cut from colored paper can be arranged on the board to cover the surface without overlapping. Use the illustration to define a tessellation. Then show several other examples using different triangles and quadrilaterals. Colored acetate pieces on the overhead projector make a vivid demonstration. Follow this introduction with the worksheets.

TRIANGLES *Sheet 1:* Show how several additional triangles can be formed using the transparency. Then have the students complete the tessellation and draw in the designs suggested.

QUADRILATERALS *Sheet 2:* Again show how several additional quadrilaterals can be formed using the transparency. Stress the importance of careful counting in constructing congruent quadrilaterals on the grid. Students should complete the tessellation with the quadrilateral before drawing in the designs.

Since the sum of the angle measures of a quadrilateral is always 360°, any quadrilateral can be used for a tessellation. Simply have the four different angles meet at a common vertex in the array. Students may illustrate this with variously shaped quadrilaterals on separate sheets of graph paper.

HEXAGONS *Sheet 3:* Illustrate and discuss carefully each of the three figures in step one. Then arrange six cutouts of the flying fish as shown and point out the hexagonal array formed from the six basic equilateral triangles.

With sheet 3 the individual student should extend the tessellation using a tracing or cutout of the original figure.

Supplementary Activities:

1. Ideally, the interested student will want to create some original tessellations on his own. Encourage this interest by posting original student designs and by illustrating other examples of Escher's works.

2. In better classes, discuss the detailed mathematical process of forming tessellations of the Escher type.

3. Students who are unfamiliar with this topic might want to explore the various regular and semiregular tessellations possible. See the references below for details.

REFERENCES

Escher, M. C. *The Graphic Work of M. C. Escher.* New York: Ballantine Books, 1967.
Ranucci, Ernest R. *Tessellation and Dissection.* Portland, Maine: J. Weston Walch, 1970.
Steinhaus, Hugo. *Mathematical Snapshots.* New York: Oxford University Press, 1969.

Editorial comment: The topic of tessellations can be introduced with a discussion of the patterns used in laying tiles on floors or building walls with bricks or blocks. Although equilateral triangles, squares, and rectangles are obvious figures for tessellations, students will be surprised to find that *all* triangles and *all* quadrilaterals, convex and concave, can be used. The suggested extension of this topic to include semiregular tessellations can be both challenging and rewarding and offers an excellent opportunity for students to explore the relationships among various regular polygons. One familiar semiregular tessellation uses regular octagons and squares. In all, eight semiregular tessellations are possible.

Congruent triangles of any shape can be used for a tessellation. They can be placed side by side to cover a surface without any overlapping and without leaving any spaces uncovered.

Step 1:   Finish covering the grid with more congruent triangles of the same size. Count squares carefully to see that each new triangle drawn is congruent to those already shown.

Step 2:   Complete the tessellation by drawing the design in alternate triangles as already begun.

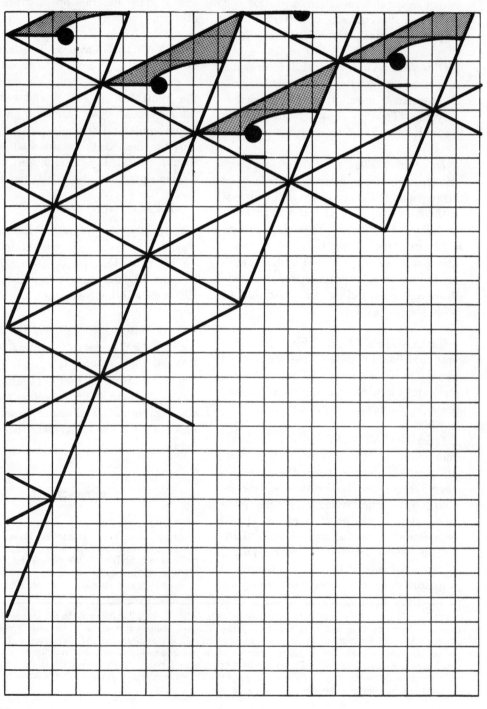

Step 1: Finish covering the grid with congruent quadrilaterals. Count squares carefully to see that each new quadrilateral drawn is congruent to those already shown.

Step 2: Now complete the tessellation by drawing the head in each quadrilateral. Notice that only half will face to the left. The other half will face to the right but be upside down.

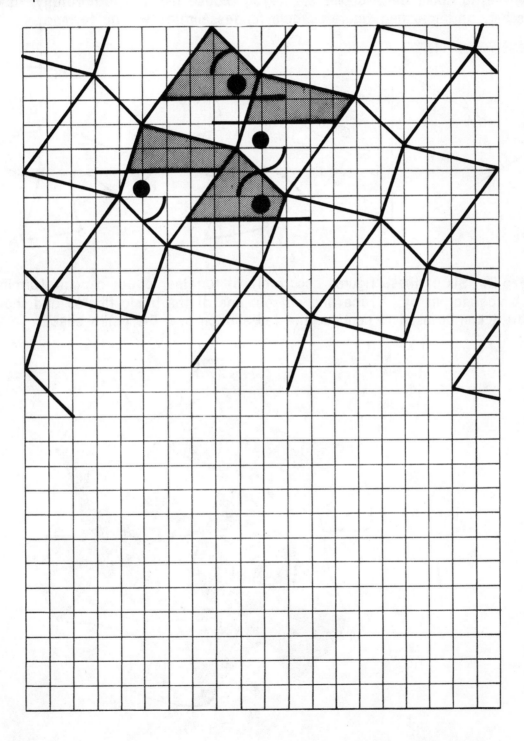

The artist M. C. Escher(1898–1972) is well known for his use of tessellations. By skillfully altering a basic polygon, such as a triangle or hexagon, he was able to produce intricate, artistic tessellations. The figure used here is based on one of Escher's drawings.

Step 1: Start with equilateral triangle ABC. Mark off the same curve on both sides AB and AC as shown. Mark off another curve on side BC that is symmetric about the midpoint P. If you choose the curves carefully, as did Escher, an interesting figure suitable for tessellating will be formed.

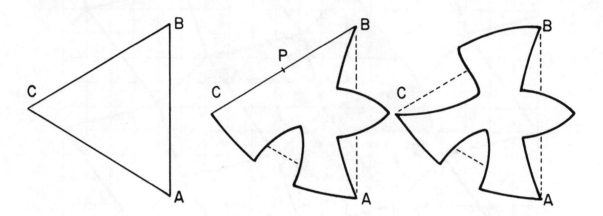

Step 2: Six of these figures accurately fit together about a point forming a hexagonal array. Trace and cut out one of the basic figures and show how it can be used to continue the tessellation over the entire sheet.

PREPARING FOR PYTHAGORAS

November 1979

By Robert A. Laing, Western Michigan University, Kalamazoo, MI 49008

Teacher's Guide

Grade level: 7–10

Materials: A set of worksheets for each student and a set of transparencies for class discussion

Objectives: To discover the relationship among the areas of similar figures constructed on the sides of right triangles. This activity together with the suggested follow-up activity should result in meaningful learning of the Pythagorean theorem.

Directions: This activity has been designed as a preliminary to the Pythagorean theorem. Sheets 1, 2, and 3 should be given as an assignment or in-class activity on the class day prior to the initial treatment of the theorem in class. Distribute copies of the three sheets to each student.

Using a transparency of sheet 1, discuss the unit of area on the isometric grid and the calculation of the sample areas. A transparency of sheet 2 may be used in a similar fashion. Note the changes to the square grid and the technique for finding areas of more difficult regions.

As an alternative technique for finding the areas on sheet 2, your students might enjoy applying Pick's rule, $A = \frac{1}{2}b + i - 1$ where b is the number of lattice points on the boundary and i is the number of interior lattice points. For an activity that permits discovery of this result, see Hirsch (1974).

Follow-up activity: After a discussion of

the students' findings on the second day, the teacher might place figure 1 on the board and ask the class how they might find the length of the shorter leg of the right triangle by using squares. After the students have attempted this problem and

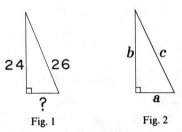

Fig. 1   Fig. 2

their results have been discussed, the class could be asked to generalize their results to find an equation that relates *a, b,* and *c* for the right triangle in figure 2.

Answers. Answers for questions 1–3 may vary depending on the order in which the areas on the legs were computed. 1. Fig. A (3, 9, 12); Fig. B (2, 6, 8); Fig. C (6, 18, 24) 2. Fig. D (2, 4½, 6½); Fig. E (2, 8, 10); Fig. F (2½, 2½, 5); Fig. G (6, 6, 12) 3. Fig. H (28.26, 50.24, 78.50) 4. (a) yes (b) yes (c) 578 5. the sum of the areas of the figures on the two legs.

BIBLIOGRAPHY

Ewbank, William A. "If Pythagoras Had a Geoboard." *Mathematics Teacher* 66 (March 1973):215–21.

Hirsch, Christian R. "Pick's Rule." *Mathematics Teacher* 67 (May 1974):431–34.

Editorial comment: The converse of the Pythagorean theorem also holds. The activity "Right or Not: A Triangle Investigation" listed at the end of this section explores this relationship.

Activities from the *Mathematics Teacher*   63

PREPARING FOR PYTHAGORAS

<u>Directions</u>: In this activity we have constructed similar figures on the three sides of right triangles. You are to find the areas of the similar figures and enter these areas in the table on Sheet 3.

1. On this sheet, the unit of area is the area of the equilateral triangle marked with an X in the sample. The area of triangle Y is also one since its area is one-half the area of rhombus Z which has two units of area.

Complete the table for Figures A-C.

Sample Areas

Figure A
Similar Equilateral Triangles

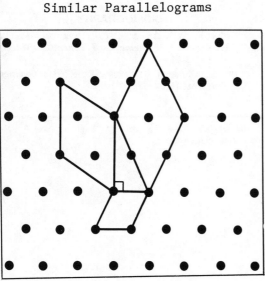

Figure B
Similar Parallelograms

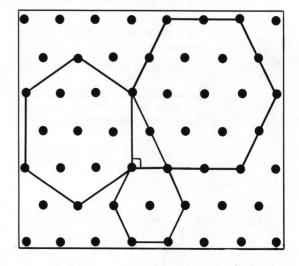

Figure C
Similar Hexagons

2. On this sheet, one unit of area will be the
area of the square marked with an X in the sample.

Sample Areas

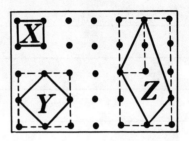

To find the areas of other figures, you can
bound the figures by rectangles as shown in the
sample. Subtract the areas of the unwanted
regions from the area of the rectangle.

Area of Y = $4 - 4(\frac{1}{2}) = 2$

Area of Z = $8 - (1 + 1 + 1/2 + 3/2) = 4$

Complete the table on Sheet 3 for Figures D-G.

Figure D
Similar Right Triangles

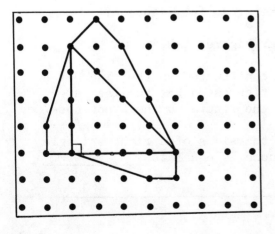

Figure E
Similar Rectangles

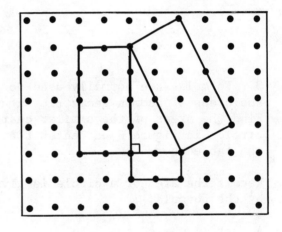

Figure F
Similar Trapezoids

Figure G
Similar Octagons

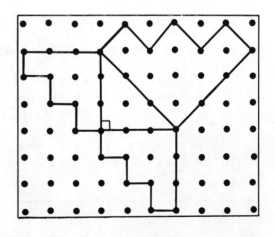

Figure	Area of Figure on One Leg	Area of Figure on Other Leg	Area of Figure on Hypotenuse
A			
B			
C			
D			
E			
F			
G			
H			

Figure H
Similar Quarter Circles

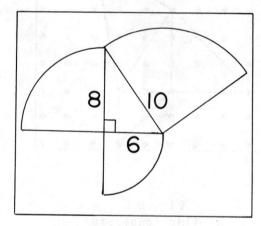

3. Formulas are normally used to find the areas of common geometric figures. Find the areas of the similar quarter circles in Figure H and enter them in the table above.

Recall the area of a circle is given by the formula:

$A = \pi r^2$, where $\pi \approx 3.14$

4. a. Do you see a relationship among the areas for Figure A?

    b. Does the same relationship hold for Figures B–H?

    c. Suppose three similar figures are constructed on the sides of a right triangle. The areas of the figures on the two legs are 128 and 450. What is the area of the figure on the hypotenuse?

5. If similar figures are constructed on the sides of a right triangle then the area of the figure on the hypotenuse is equal to _____

PYTHAGOREAN PUZZLES

February 1974

By Raymond E. Spaulding, Radford College
Radford, Virginia

Teacher's Guide

Grade level: 7–10

Materials: Scissors and duplicate copies of the three worksheets

Objective: To enable students to discover demonstrations of the Pythagorean theorem in puzzle format

Directions: Distribute the set of puzzles and a pair of scissors to each student.

Sheet 1: First discuss with the students how squares A and B have been constructed on the legs of the right triangle and square C on its hypotenuse. Explain that the areas of these three squares can be represented as a^2, b^2, and c^2 respectively. Also describe how square B has been subdivided. Next let each student cut out square A and the four pieces of square B and try to arrange them so square C is covered.

Sheet 2: Before any cutting, each student should check to see that squares A, B, and C are equal in length to the sides a, b, and c of the right triangle cut from sheet 1. Also the student should show that the triangle is congruent to the two right triangles indicated on squares A and B. Next let each student cut out the five pieces from squares A and B and try to arrange them so square C is covered.

Sheet 3: Before cutting, each student should compare sides a, b, and c of the three squares with sides a, b, and c of the right triangle cut from sheet 1. Also the student should show that the four right

triangles indicated on square C are congruent to the one cut from sheet 1. Next let each student cut out the five pieces from square C and try to arrange them so squares A and B are covered.

Allow each student plenty of time to find a solution to each puzzle. Students can then effectively display their solutions on an overhead projector using pieces of colored acetate. Use each solution to show how the puzzle demonstrates that $a^2 + b^2 = c^2$.

These puzzles can create interest, enthusiasm, and problem-solving experiences for students. The depth of mathematical involvement will vary at different grade levels. At the junior high level, they provide problem-solving tasks that demonstrate geometrically the Pythagorean theorem. At a higher level these same puzzles can suggest a variety of geometric and algebraic proofs.

Supplementary activity:

Have your students try the same puzzles again using other right triangles of their own choice along with the corresponding squares.

REFERENCE

Loomis, Elisha S. *The Pythagorean Proposition.* Washington, D.C.: National Council of Teachers of Mathematics, 1968.

Puzzles 1, 2, and 3 are taken respectively from proofs 9, 165, and 225. Algebraic proofs 231 and 33 follow directly. Similar activities can be designed from other proofs.

Editorial comment: Sometimes the most meaningful type of experience involving a theorem in geometry is a hands-on activity with physical objects. Although not proofs in the formal sense, these Pythagorean activities may well be more convincing than any rigorous, logical mathematical argument of this famous theorem. An impressive display of the applicability of this theorem to all right triangles can be made by having students repeat the first puzzle with a right triangle of their own choice. Further reinforcement can be gained by exploring a similar activity involving areas for triangles that are *not* right triangles. Keep the longest side fixed but change the right angle to form an acute triangle. The areas of the squares on the two shorter sides, when combined, will be *more* than that of the square on the longest side. If the right angle is changed to form an obtuse triangle, the areas of the squares on the two shorter sides, when combined, will be *less* than that on the longest side.

1. Cut out square A and the four pieces from square B.

2. Show how the pieces can be arranged to cover square C.

3. Does $a^2 + b^2$ appear to equal c^2? Why?

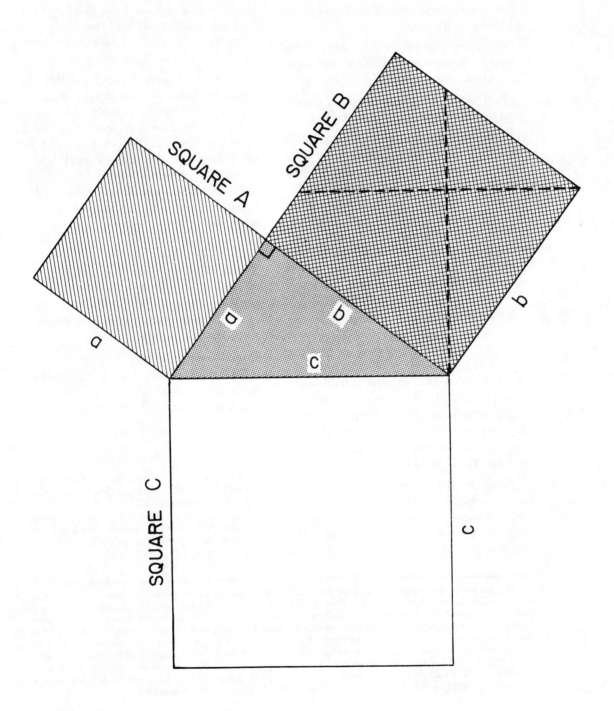

PYTHAGOREAN PUZZLE: Sheet 2   NAME_____

1. Cut out the five pieces from squares A and B.

2. Show how the pieces can be arranged to cover square C.

3. Does $a^2 + b^2$ appear to equal c^2? Why?

SQUARE C

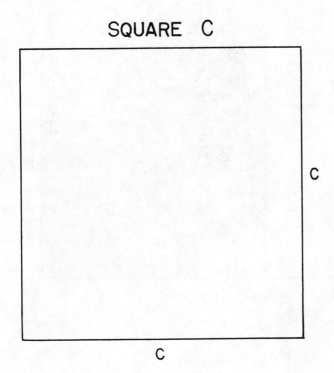

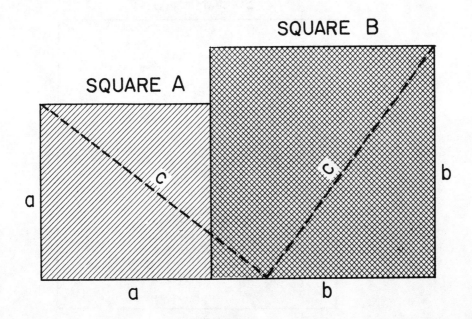

NAME————————————

1. Cut out the five pieces from square C.

2. Show how the pieces can be arranged to cover squares A and B.

3. Does $a^2 + b^2$ appear to equal c^2? Why?

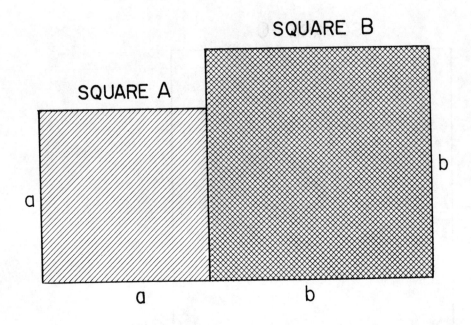

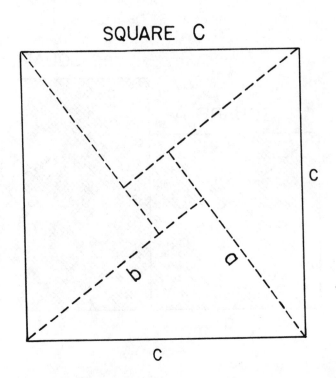

POLYHEDRA FROM CARDBOARD AND ELASTICS

April 1977

By John Woolaver, Hillside Intermediate School, Salt Lake City, UT 84108

For years teachers and students have labored to construct models of regular and semiregular polyhedra using cardboard and glue. It is considerably easier to eliminate the glue and substitute elastics [rubber bands]. All the Platonic and Archimedean solids can be quickly assembled and disassembled if sufficient cardboard faces and elastics are available.

Teacher's Guide

Grade level: 7–12

Materials: One set of worksheets for each student, cardboard, and elastics

Objectives: To provide an optional take-home project for students that will acquaint them with a few of the well-known polyhedra

Directions: Present a brief history of the five Platonic solids, emphasizing that they were studied by the Greeks as early as 400 B.C. Mention that the ancient philosophers knew only four elements—fire, earth, air, and water—and that they associated these four elements with four of the Platonic solids, namely, tetrahedron (fire), hexahedron (earth), octahedron (air), and icosahedron (water). The fifth Platonic solid, dodecahedron, was thought to represent the shape of the universe. Distribute worksheets to each student instructing them to cut the faces from easy-folding cardboard similar to file folders. An assortment of colored cardboard can be used for more attractive polyhedra. Elastics for assembling the polygons should be slightly shorter than the edges of the polygons. Larger or smaller polyhedra can be made by varying the size of the polygons. Suggest that the students work together if they so desire.

REFERENCES

Boyer, Carl B. *A History of Mathematics.* New York: John Wiley & Sons, 1968.

Jacobs, Harold R. *Mathematics: A Human Endeavor.* San Francisco: W. H. Freeman & Co., 1970.

Prichett, Gordon D. "Three-Dimensional Discovery." *Mathematics Teacher* 69 (January 1976):5–10.

Wenninger, Magnus J. *Polyhedron Models for the Classroom.* 2d ed. Reston, Va.: National Council of Teachers of Mathematics, 1975.

Editorial comment: The fact that there are exactly five regular polyhedra can be established as follows. Assume that there exists a regular polyhedron with each face a regular n-gon and that there are p of these polygons at each vertex. Since the degree measure of each angle of a regular polygon is $180(n-2)/n$, the sum of the measures around each vertex is $p[180(n-2)/n]$. Since the faces do not lie in the same plane, $p[180(n-2)/n] < 360$. Elementary algebra can now be used to find all possible integral solutions for n and p.

Activities from the *Mathematics Teacher* 71

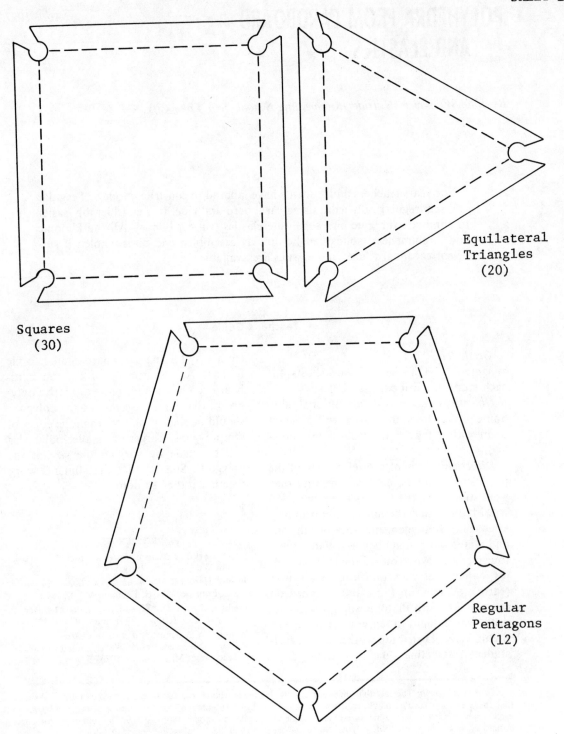

Squares
(30)

Equilateral
Triangles
(20)

Regular
Pentagons
(12)

<u>Instructions</u>: Copy patterns on appropriate cardboard. All broken-line
segments are 6 cm long, center to center.

Cut out the patterns. If all models are to be constructed, you will need
thirty squares, twenty triangles, and twelve pentagons. Punch out all
holes with a small paper punch. Cut out slots to each hole. Fold along
broken lines between holes. Score first for accurate folding.

Tetrahedron
(fire)

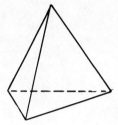

Hexahedron
(earth)

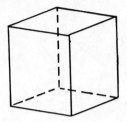

Octahedron
(air)

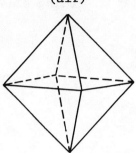

Icosahedron
(water)

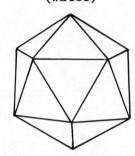

Dodecahedron
(universe)

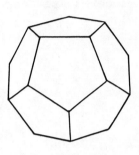

The five solids shown above are the only <u>regular</u> solids that can be constructed. They are referred to as the Platonic solids, named after the ancient Greek philosopher Plato. A regular solid is one in which all faces, edges, and angles are congruent. You can construct the Platonic solids using the appropriate number of polygons as listed below:

1. Tetrahedron (4 triangles)

2. Hexahedron (6 squares)

3. Octahedron (8 triangles)

4. Dodecahedron (12 pentagons)

5. Icosahedron (20 triangles)

After completing these solids, see if you can discover why only five regular solids can be made. Remember, all faces of a regular solid must be regular polygons of the same size and shape.

Step 1. Using elastics, attach a square to each side of a pentagon as
         shown.

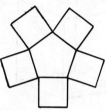

Step 2. Attach triangles between the squares as shown. This will result
         in a saucer-shaped assembly.

Step 3. Attach a pentagon to a square as shown.

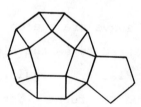

Step 4. Attach squares to the four remaining sides of the pentagon just
         attached. Then attach triangles as needed to fill in the spaces
         between the squares.

Step 5. Repeat steps 3 and 4 as needed to complete the assembly.

A semiregular solid has several regular polygons of different shapes
as faces. The rhombicosidodecahedron you have just assembled is one such
semiregular solid. It is a member of the set referred to as the Archimedean solids. Perhaps you can do some research and construct the other
Archimedean solids.

POINSOT STARS

January 1980

By Christian R. Hirsch, Western Michigan University, Kalamazoo, MI 49008

Teacher's Guide

Grade Level: 6–10.

Materials: One set of activity sheets, a ruler, and tracing paper for each student, and a set of transparencies of the activity sheets for class discussion.

Objectives: Students will discover the following generalizations: The number of Poinsot stars determined by n equally spaced points on a circle is $n/2$ if n is even or $(n-1)/2$ if n is odd. The number of regular Poinsot stars determined by n points is the number of positive integers less than or equal to $n/2$ and relatively prime to n. In particular, if n is prime, then the number of regular Poinsot stars is $(n-1)/2$. If each of n equally spaced points on a circle is connected to every dth point with a line segment, the resulting Poinsot star is regular, provided n and d are relatively prime.

Procedure: Distribute activity sheets to each student. The star-shaped figures obtained in this activity were first studied systematically by the French mathematician Louis Poinsot (pwan.sō) in 1809 and are thus called Poinsot stars (Davis and Chinn 1969). Note that two Poinsot stars are considered the same if and only if they are congruent. In the process of completing the table on sheet 1, some students will discover that for n equally spaced points on a circle, the Poinsot star formed by connecting every dth point is the same as that obtained by connecting every $(n-d)$th point. You may wish to discuss this generalization with the entire class. An immediate consequence of this fact is the generalization that the number of Poinsot stars determined by n points is equal to the number of distinct ways in which n can be represented as the sum of two positive integers.

Note that for n equally spaced points on a circle, one of the regular Poinsot stars is the regular convex n-gon. The remaining regular Poinsot stars are n-sided nonsimple polygons. However, each of these is "regular" in the sense that all n sides are congruent as are all n vertex angles (angles whose vertices are on the circle).

Supplementary Activities: An investigation of the nonregular Poinsot stars determined by n points can produce several interesting conjectures relating the simple closed paths that comprise the star, the number of orbits around the circle in completing these paths, and the greatest common divisor or the least common multiple of n and the number d of spaces between connected points. For a discussion of these results see Bennett (1978).

Students who have had an introduction to symmetry might be encouraged to analyze their regular Poinsot stars for line and rotational symmetry. Others might be encouraged to generate artistic designs by superimposing various combinations of the Poinsot stars determined by a given number of points. For example, if all the Poinsot starts determined by twenty-four points are drawn on a circle, an illusion of a series of concentric circles is created.

Some students might be challenged to use multiplication tables for modular arithmetics to determine which of n equally spaced points on a circle are to be connected. This will result in some very interesting art as well as mathematics. A discussion of this technique can be found in Locke (1972).

Answers: 4b. Yes; 5b. Yes; 7. 2, 2, 3, 3, 4, 4, 5, 5, 6; 8. 7, 13; 9. $n/2$ if n is even, $(n-1)/2$ if n is odd; 10. 1, 2, 1, 3, 2, 3, 2, 5, 2; 11. They are prime numbers. 12. 6; 13. $(n-1)/2$; 14. 1, 2, 1, 3, 2, 3, 2, 5, 2; 15. 4, 14; 16. Yes; 17. The number of positive integers $\leq n/2$ and relatively prime to n. 18. n and d must be relatively prime.

REFERENCES

Bennett, Albert. "Star Patterns." *Arithmetic Teacher* 25 (January 1978): 12–14.

Davis, Philip, and William Chinn. *3.1416 and All That.* New York: Simon and Schuster, 1969.

Locke, Phil. "Residue Designs." *Mathematics Teacher* 65 (March 1972): 260–63.

Editorial comment: You may wish to follow up this activity with a discussion of curve stitching. Have students place and number thirty-six equally spaced points around a circle drawn on posterboard. Use yarn or colored thread to connect each point n to $2n$ with a stitch. (Consider 37 equivalent to 1, 38 to 2, and so on.) The yarn (thread) should be started from the back of the posterboard and pushed through point 1 with a needle and then stitched to point 2. Pupils could also investigate the design formed by connecting each point n to $3n$ (or n to $4n$). The resulting designs make very attractive bulletin board displays.

On each circle below, 6 equally spaced points have been marked.

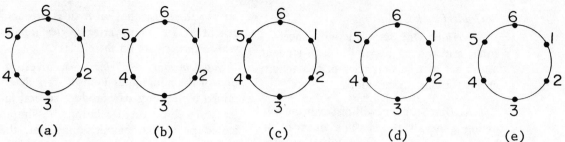

(a)   (b)   (c)   (d)   (e)

1. On circle (a), connect consecutive points with line segments,

   beginning at point 1.

2. Beginning with point 1, connect each point on circle (b) to every

   second point with a line segment.

3. Connect each point on circle (c) to every third point.

4. a. Connect each point on circle (d) to every fourth point.

   b. Is the figure you obtained the same as a previous figure?

5. a. Connect each point on circle (e) to every fifth point.

   b. Is this figure the same as one of the previous figures?

The figures you obtained above are called <u>Poinsot</u> (pwan.sō) <u>stars</u>.

For 6 equally spaced points on a circle there are exactly 3 different

Poinsot stars.

6. Show that for 4

   points there are

   exactly 2 different

   Poinsot stars.

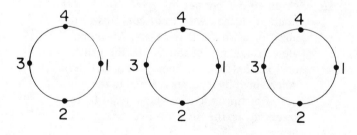

7. Complete the table below by tracing onto a sheet of paper copies

   of the appropriate circle on sheet 2.

Number of points ($\underline{n}$)	4	5	6	7	8	9	10	11	12
Number of Poinsot stars	2		3						

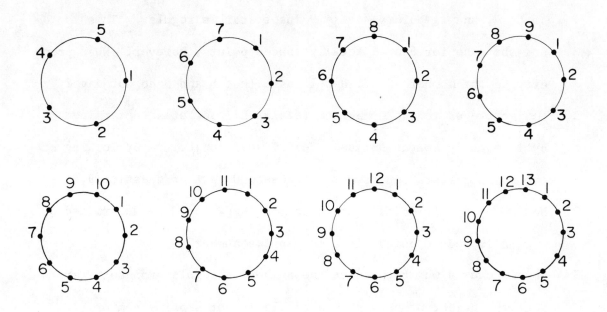

8. Study your results. Conjecture as to the number of different

   Poinsot stars determined by 14 equally spaced points. By 27

   equally spaced points.

9. How many Poinsot stars do you think would be determined by $\underline{n}$

   equally spaced points? Check your conjecture for $\underline{n}$ = 13.

A Poinsot star is called <u>regular</u> if it can be drawn without lifting

your pencil from the paper. On sheet 1 you saw that 3 Poinsot stars

were determined by 6 points. Of these 3, only the first one you drew

was a regular Poinsot star.

10. Using the Poinsot stars you obtained for question 7, complete the

    table below.

Number of points (n)	4	5	6	7	8	9	10	11	12
Number of regular Poinsot stars			1						

11. Compare your tables on sheets 1 and 2. Observe that for the cases of 5, 7, and 11 points, _every_ Poinsot star is regular. This is not the case for 8 or 9 equally spaced points, however. What property do the numbers 5, 7, and 11 have that 8 and 9 do not have?

12. Conjecture as to the number of regular Poinsot stars determined by 13 equally spaced points. Verify your conjecture by looking at the Poinsot stars you drew for the second part of question 9.

13. How many regular Poinsot stars do you think would be determined by _n_ equally spaced points if _n_ is a prime number?

14. To discover a way to predict the number of regular Poinsot stars when the number of points on a circle is not a prime number, complete the following table. Recall that two positive integers are relatively prime if their only common factor is 1.

Number of points (n)	4	5	6	7	8	9	10	11	12
Number of positive integers $\leq n/2$ and relatively prime to n	1								

15. Compare the table above with that on sheet 2. Using the table above, predict the number of regular Poinsot stars determined by 24 equally spaced points on a circle. By 29 equally spaced points.

16. Is your answer for the second part of question 15 consistent with your answer to question 13?

17. How many regular Poinsot stars do you think would be determined by _n_ equally spaced points?

18. Suppose _n_ equally spaced points are marked on a circle. Then each point is connected to every _d_th point with a line segment. What numerical relationship must exist between _n_ and _d_ if the resulting Poinsot star is to be regular?

CONICS FROM STRAIGHT LINES AND CIRCLES: PARABOLAS

March 1973

By Evan M. Maletsky, Montclair State College, Upper Montclair, NJ 07043

Teacher's Guide

Grade level: 7–12

Materials: One parabola worksheet for each student, as well as a transparency for class discussion and demonstration

Objective: To give a simple construction for a family of parabolas

Directions: Distribute a worksheet to each student.

On the transparency mark the point on both line 1 and circle 1. Then mark the two points on both line 2 and circle 2. Discuss how far these two points are from line 0 and the center of the circles.

Now have the students mark these same points on their worksheets along with the pairs of points on line 3 and circle 3, line 4 and circle 4, and so on. Ask them to connect the points with a smooth curve and describe what they get.

Mark the same points on the transparency and draw the *parabola*. Note to the class that for every point on the parabola the distance to line 0 is equal to the distance to the center of the circles.

Using a different color, mark all points on the transparency for which the distance to line −1 is equal to the distance to the center of the circles. Connect these points to show another parabola.

Now have the students draw on their worksheets all the other parabolas they can find in a similar fashion.

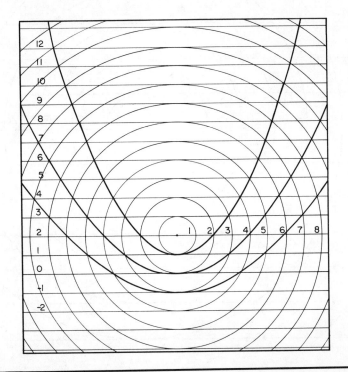

Editorial comment: This activity reinforces the locus definition of a parabola: the set of all points equidistant from a point (focus) and line (directrix). Although all parabolas that can be drawn on the worksheet have the same focal point, each has a different directrix. The sharper the curve is, the closer the focal point is to the line.

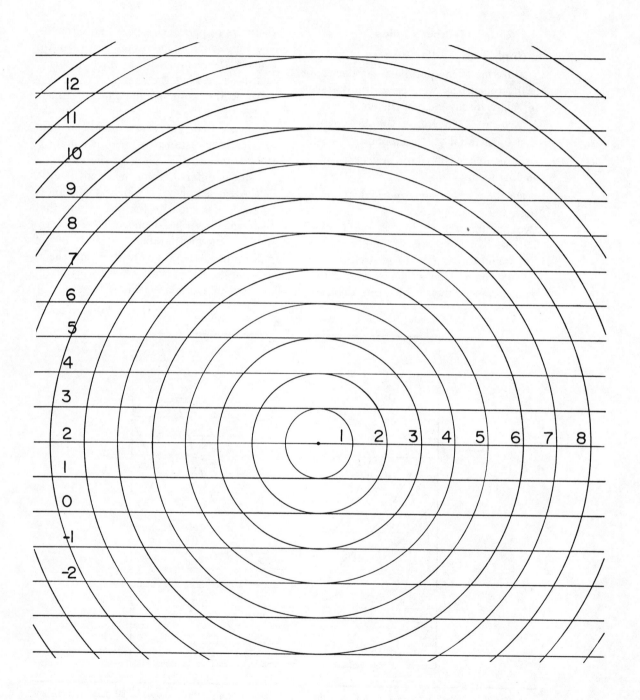

CONICS FROM STRAIGHT LINES AND CIRCLES: ELLIPSES AND HYPERBOLAS

Teacher's Guide

Grade level: **7–12**

Materials: Two worksheets for each student, as well as two transparencies for class discussion and demonstration

Objective: To give simple constructions for a family of ellipses and a family of hyperbolas

Directions for ellipses: Distribute a worksheet to each student.

On a transparency have a student mark as many points as he can find such that the numbers of the two corresponding circles add to 12: for example, circles 1 and 11, circles 2 and 10, and circles 3 and 9.

Have each student copy these points on his worksheet and connect them with a smooth curve. Draw the *ellipse* on the transparency, as well. Note to the class that the sum of the distances from each point on the ellipse to the two centers (foci) is always 12.

Now see if your students can find other ellipses in a similar fashion. For example, try sums of 13, 14, and 15.

Directions for hyperbolas: Using another worksheet and transparency, repeat the same process. But this time start with points on the circles with numbers that differ by 6: for example, circles 8 and 2, circles 9 and 3, and circles 10 and 4. Draw the corresponding *hyperbola* and see how many others your students can find.

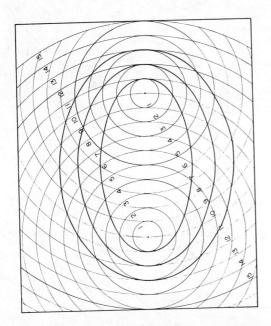 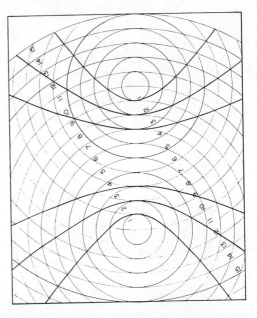

Editorial comment: This activity reinforces the locus definition of an ellipse and a hyperbola. When the *sum* of the distances from two fixed points is constant, the curve is an ellipse. For the two foci given on the worksheet, as the sum increases, the ellipse becomes more circular. When the *difference* of the distances between two fixed points is constant, the curve is a hyperbola. For the two foci given on the worksheet, as the difference increases, the hyperbola bends more sharply around the points.

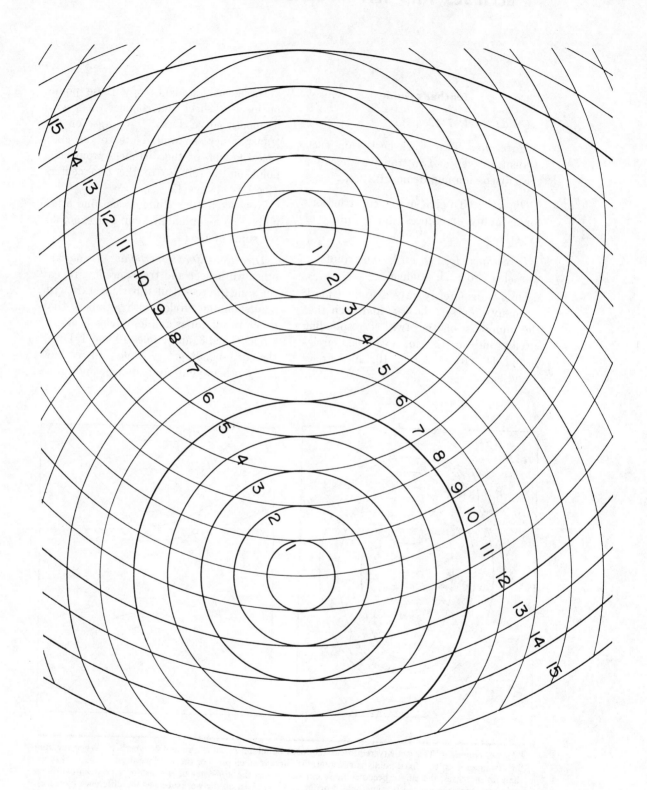

Additional Activities for
Geometry

Allen, Charles E. "Mission—Construction." Nov. 1972, 631–34. Pupils follow step-by-step procedures to construct the circumcenter, centroid, orthocenter, and incenter of an acute triangle and then use their results to discover the nine-point circle theorem. (Grades 7–12)

Allen, Charles E. "Mission—Tangrams" (Part 1 and Part 2). Feb. 1973, 143–46. Students follow detailed directions to graph points on a coordinate system and connect them to form the pieces of a tangram puzzle. Using all seven pieces, they then try to duplicate various polygonal shapes and form letters of the alphabet. (Grades 7–12)

Bolster, L. Carey. "Tessellations." Apr. 1973, 339–42. Using cutout shapes, students determine which regular polygons can be used to tessellate a plane. They also investigate tile designs that can be made using different combinations of regular polygons. (Grades 7–9)

Maletsky, Evan M. "Fun with Flips." Oct. 1973, 531–34. Students visualize flipping triangles, squares, and rectangles end over end along a line and then indicate the positions of reference arrows or sketch the paths of points marked on the figures as they are flipped from one position to another. (Grades 7–10)

Maletsky, Evan M. "Patterns and Positions." Dec. 1973, 723–26. Pupils visualize which patterns of six squares can be folded to form a cube and complete the coloring or identify the location of various faces on patterns so as to match assembled cubes. (Grades 7–10)

Smith, Stanley A. "Rolling Curves." Mar. 1974, 239–42. Students construct several curves of constant width and demonstrate that cardboard models "roll" evenly. (Grades 8–9)

Masalski, William J. "Midpoints and Quadrilaterals." Jan. 1975, 37–38, 43–44. Students discover the relationship of a quadrilateral and its perimeter to that of the figure determined by the midpoints of the line segments from the vertices of the quadrilateral to any other point in the plane of the quadrilateral. They also explore relationships between a quadrilateral and the figure determined by the midpoints of the sides of the quadrilateral. (Grades 7–9)

Jamski, William. "Some Properties of Regular Polygons." Mar. 1975, 213–14, 219–20. Students discover generalizations involving the measures of the interior and exterior angles of regular polygons by organizing data in a table and looking for patterns. (Grades 8–10)

Bolster, L. Carey. "Tangram Mathematics." Feb. 1977, 143–46. Pupils cut out a tangram puzzle and use the pieces to create geometric shapes and determine area relationships. (Grades 7–10)

Roberge, James J. "Tangram Geometry." Mar. 1977, 239–42. Students use pieces of a cutout tangram puzzle two at a time, three at a time, and so on up to seven at a time to create common geometric shapes. A ruler and protractor are then used to determine properties of those shapes that are convex quadrilaterals. (Grades 7–10)

Smith, Stanley A. "Taxi Distance." May 1977, 431–34. Students find taxi distances between pairs of points and determine the loci of points equitaxidistant from a given point and from two given points. (Grades 7–10)

Hirsch, Christian R. "Painting Polyhedra." Feb. 1978, 119–22. Pupils discover Euler's formula relating the numbers of faces, vertices, and edges of polyhedra and solve combinatorial problems involving painting vertices and edges of a tetrahedron and a hexahedron using two colors. (Grades 7–10)

Freitag, Richard A. "Tiling." Mar. 1978, 199–202. Students form polygons (replications) from cutout congruent parts so that the whole figure is similar to each part. They also identify the congruent replicas in given replications. (Grades 7–12)

Spaulding, Raymond E. "Tetrahexes." Oct. 1978, 598–602. Pupils determine the number of different polygonal shapes (trihexes) that can be formed by three congruent regular hexagons that must match up along common sides. They also investigate the number of polygonal shapes (tetrahexes) that can be made from four hexagons. The tetrahexes are then analyzed for line and rotational symmetry and are used to reproduce given designs. These designs are subsequently analyzed for their symmetry. (Grades 7–10)

Butler, Ruth. "Faces of a Cube." Mar. 1979, 199–202. Pupils visualize folding and rotating cubes and sketch and identify the polygonal shapes formed when a cube is cut by a plane. (Grades 7–10)

Dolan, Daniel T. "Right or Not: A Triangle Investigation." Apr. 1979, 279–82. Students investigate the relationship between the lengths of the sides of a triangle and its classification by angle by constructing and measuring triangles whose sides are edges of squares cut from centimeter grid paper. (Grades 8–12)

Daunis, Geraldine. "Polyhedra Planar Projection." Sept. 1979, 438–43. Geometric perception is used to identify and sketch projections of polyhedra onto one of their faces. (Grades 7–12)

Davis, Edward J., and Don Thompson. "Sectioning a Regular Tetrahedron." Feb. 1980, 121–25. Pupils visualize and sketch cross sections formed by a plane cutting a regular tetrahedron through a vertex, along an edge, and through a face and then examine characteristics of the resulting polyhedra. (Grades 8 and up)

Olson, Melfried. "Beyond the Usual Constructions." May 1980, 361–64. Basic constructions (bisecting angles, constructing a perpendicular from a point to a line, and constructing the perpendicular bisector of a segment) are used to explore special points and lines, such as the Fermat point and the Simson line, in an acute triangle. (Grades 7–12)

Meneeley, Merrill A. "Graphing—Perimeter—Area." Sept. 1980, 441–44. Students review the plotting of points on a Cartesian coordinate system and then draw and identify polygons with given points as vertices or polygons which form the boundary of the intersection of four linear inequalities. Perimeters and areas of these polygons are computed. (Grades 7–10)

Activities for
Measurement

It is essential not only that students learn how to measure and how to compute with measurements but also that they maintain these skills throughout their educational training in mathematics. Activities such as those included in this section offer a good opportunity to reinforce measurement skills in a variety of ways.

The first activity, "Centimeter and Millimeter Measurements," begins with estimating and then advances to measuring. The first worksheet contains a centimeter scale calibrated in millimeters that can be cut out and used as a ruler. The second worksheet gives a paper cutout for a small metric caliper that can be used with surprising accuracy. "Pedaling Mathematics" is an activity that deals with applications of mathematics in a bicycle. A variety of actual bicycle measurements are called for—tire circumference and related diameter, and gear ratios explored by measuring diameters and counting teeth.

The activity "Pick's Rule" begins with a discovery relating the number of boundary and interior points of special polygons drawn on a grid with their corresponding areas. This interesting theorem is then applied in finding the areas of a variety of such polygons. "Volume and Surface Area" is an activity that investigates the volume and surface area of a box that can be formed from a rectangular piece of paper with squares of equal areas cut from its corners. As the size of the squares changes, so do the volume and surface area of the box. Students make the models first, estimate, and then compute.

This section ends with an application activity, "Area and Cost per Unit." Polygons representing the boundaries of tent floors serve as the basis for finding areas, sometimes by partitioning. These areas and the corresponding tent costs are then used to find and compare the cost per unit area. The last worksheet requires finding the total area of a tent formed from seven different polygons.

Additional activities that are primarily measurement oriented are listed at the end of this section.

CENTIMETER AND MILLIMETER MEASUREMENTS

November 1974

By L. Carey Bolster, Baltimore County Public Schools, Towson, Maryland

Teacher's Guide

Grade level: 7–8

Materials: Scissors and copies of sheets 1–3

Objectives: Students will estimate lengths to the nearest centimeter and millimeter, then measure and find the error between their estimates and actual measures.

Procedure: Make copies of student worksheets 1–3.

Sheet 1: Before distributing sheet 1, students should have some idea about the relationship of a centimeter and millimeter. Students should guess the length of each of the five segments to the nearest centimeter and millimeter and enter their estimate in the appropriate table. Then students should cut out the ruler and make the actual measures. Be sure they measure to the nearest centimeter or millimeter as indicated.

Sheets 2 and 3: Distribute sheets 2 and 3 to the students. Have them follow the directions for cutting out and assembling the metric caliper. In order to show how to measure using the metric caliper, you may wish to make a transparency for use on the overhead. Be sure that students understand what is meant by "to the nearest tenth of a centimeter." This lesson could be extended greatly by providing additional objects for students to measure.

Note. Since some methods of duplicating will distort the scales that are provided, no answers are given here for sheet 1. Answers for the "Actual Measure" column should be provided by using one of the duplicated rulers. Answers in the "Estimate" and "Error" columns will vary for different students.

Editorial comment: The activity on the first worksheet could be extended by noting that the ruler provided is 2 decimeters long. Ask pupils to estimate and then measure in decimeters their height, the width of a desk, the height of their classroom, and perhaps some dimensions related to the chalkboard.

You may find it preferable to copy worksheet 2 on tagboard or cardboard the weight of a file folder. Careful construction will produce an accurate metric caliper. If a real metric caliper with a vernier is available, this would be a good time to bring it in, describe its use, and note how accurately it can measure.

Estimating Lengths to Nearest Centimeter and Millimeter

Cut out this ruler
to make measures

Estimate the length of each of these segments
to the nearest centimeter and then to the nearest
millimeter. Enter your estimate in the tables
below. Then measure each segment and enter
the actual measure in the table. In the "Error"
column place a + sign in front of error if the
estimate is larger than actual measure. Place
a − sign in front of error if estimate is smaller
than actual measure.

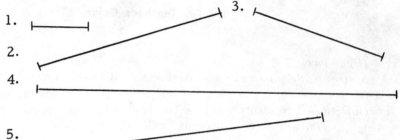

1.

2.

3.

4.

5.

Nearest Centimeter

Segment	Estimate	Actual Measure	Error
1			
2			
3			
4			
5			

Nearest Millimeter

Segment	Estimate	Actual Measure	Error
1			
2			
3			
4			
5			

Bonus

Estimate the total length of these coins to the
nearest millimeter if they are placed as shown.
Measure to test your guess.

METRIC CALIPER

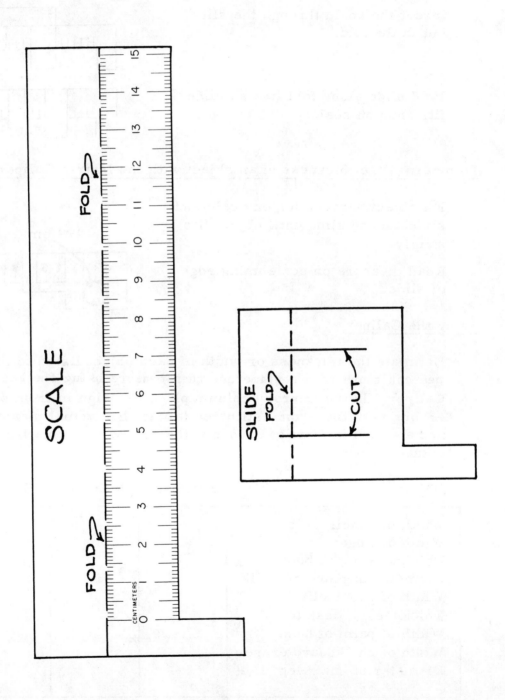

METRIC CALIPER

Constructing the Metric Caliper

Carefully cut out the slide and scale.
Fold the scale as shown.

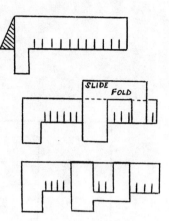

Insert the scale through the slits
cut in the slide.

Fold slide along fold line so slide
fits snug on scale.

To measure the thickness of an object with the Metric Caliper

Fit object between leg on scale and
slide.   Push slide until object fits
snugly.

Read measure on scale using edge
of slide.

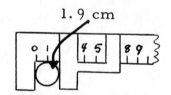

Using the Caliper

Estimate the thickness or width of each object listed to the
nearest tenth of a centimeter; then measure using the Metric
Caliper.   In the "Error" column place a + sign in front of
errors resulting from estimates larger than actual measures
and a - sign in front of errors if the estimate is smaller than
actual measures.

Object	Estimate	Measure	Error
Width of pencil			
Width of finger			
Thickness of textbook			
Diameter of piece of chalk			
Width of paper clip			
Thickness of desk top			
Width of palm of hand			
Width of chalkboard eraser			
Diameter of chair leg			

PEDALING MATHEMATICS

October 1975

By James R. Metz, Griffin High School, Springfield, Illinois

Teacher's Guide

Grade level: 7–9

Materials: One or more bicycles, a set of worksheets for each student, and rulers and protractors

Objectives: Students will measure lengths and angles of certain parts of a bicycle as described by diagrams and solve problems based on these measurements.

Directions: This is recommended as an outdoor activity but could be done in the classroom if necessary. Have students work in small groups with an assortment of bicycles, including a 10-speed, so different results can be compared. Distribute the worksheets one at a time. Metric measurement may be used, but most tires and other standard dimensions will be in customary U.S. units.

Comments: Answers will depend upon the type and size of the bicycles used.

Sheet 1: Encourage accurate measuring. Relate seat and head angles of the same size to parallel parts of the frame. Professionals suggest the best seat adjustment is 109 percent of the rider's inseam measurement. However, many riders believe this to be too high for comfort.

Sheet 2: Have students use their own methods to measure the tire circumference. Tire size is outside diameter × tire width. An interesting additional activity is the tracing out of a cycloid. Place the bicycle against the wall and trace out the path of a point on the tire, starting at the floor, as the bicycle is rolled forward.

Sheet 3: Careful counting and measuring are critical for correct proportions. Typical gear numbers for single-speed bicycles are around 70. For 10-speed bikes the gear numbers range from around 35 to 100.

REFERENCE

Cuthbertson, Thomas. *Bike Tripping*. Berkeley, Calif.: Ten Speed Press, 1972.

Editorial comment: Much of the teaching of measurment centers on how to read measurement scales. But students also need practice in the proper use of rulers and protractors. This activity offers valuable experience in handling these measuring tools to measure the distances and angles described in a diagram. Be sure your students develop competence in this basic skill.

Although the activity is designed for use in a mathematics class during school, it can also be an interesting homework assignment. An activity related to worksheet 3 might be to examine how the hands of a clock are geared so that the minute hand moves around twelve times for each revolution of the hour hand. Better students might want to design such a gear system on their own rather than examine one. This requires a working knowledge of gear ratios. Be sure they take note that each hand moves about the same center and in a clockwise direction.

Carefully measure each dimension on the bicycle, using a ruler.

1. frame size _____   4. fork rake _____

2. wheel base _____   5. drop _____

3. top tube _____   6. chain stay _____

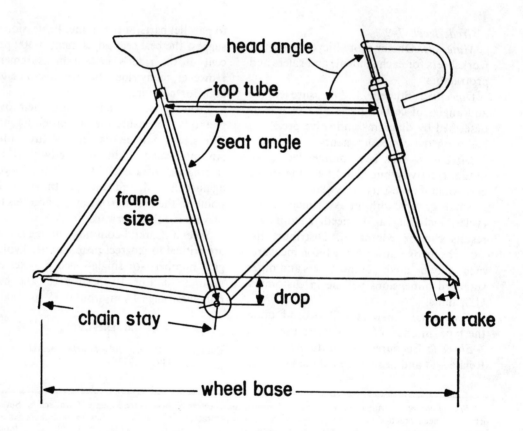

7. Measure the seat angle and the head angle   _____
   using a protractor. Are they the same size?
                                                  _____

8. Measure the seat height from the top of the
   saddle to the pedal in its lowest position.   _____

1. Carefully measure each dimension on the bicycle.

        spoke length   _____

        wheel radius   _____

        outside tire diameter   _____

        tire width   _____

        tire circumference   _____

2. Read the two numbers on your bicycle tire that
    give the tire size. What does each number   _____ x _____
    measure?

3. Compute the circumference of the tire using
    the measured tire diameter and the formula   _____

            C = πd.

    How does your answer compare with the
    measured circumference?   _____

4. How far would the bicycle travel in 100 tire
    revolutions?   _____

    How many tire revolutions would be needed to
    travel a mile?   _____

    At 120 tire revolutions per minute, how long
    would it take to travel a mile?   _____

The bicycle chain transmits the pedal
motion from the front driving sprocket
to the rear wheel sprocket.

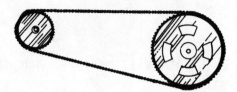

1. Count the number of teeth in the driving
    sprocket (T) and the rear wheel sprocket (t).
    Use the largest front and smallest rear
    sprockets if there are more than one on
    either end.

    T = _____

    t = _____

2. Measure the diameter of the drive sprocket (D)
    and the rear wheel sprocket (d).

    D = _____

    d = _____

3. Turn the pedals for 20 complete revolutions (R)
    and count the number of turns made by the
    rear wheel (r).

    R = ____20____

    r = _____

4. The values of R and r are related by this
    formula. Use it to compute the number of
    revolutions (r) made by the rear wheel if
    the pedal makes 20 revolutions (R).

    $$TR = tr$$

    How does this number compare with your answer
    to question 3?

    _____

5. The values of R and r are also related by this
    formula. Use it to compute r for an R value
    of 20.

    $$DR = dr$$

    How does this number compare with your answer
    to question 3?

    _____

6. The gear number of a bicycle is the diameter
    of the tire required if the pedals were
    attached directly to the wheel. It can be
    found using this formula.

    $$\frac{\text{Gear}}{\text{Number}} = \frac{T}{t} \times \text{tire diameter}$$

    Find the gear number for your bicycle. If you
    have a 10-speed bike, see if you can compute
    the gear numbers for all 10 settings of the
    shift lever.

    _____

PICK'S RULE

May 1974

By Christian R. Hirsch
Western Michigan University, Kalamazoo, Michigan

Teacher's Guide

Grade level: 7–10

Materials: One set of worksheets for each student and a set of transparencies for class discussion

Objectives: The student will discover and apply Pick's theorem for finding the area of a polygon whose vertices are lattice points.

Directions: Distribute the worksheets one at a time. Be sure to allow sufficient time so that each student has had an opportunity to discover the rule for himself.

Have students discuss their answers after they have completed sheet 2. A complete set of answers can be given on the transparencies.

Sheet 3 will provide opportunities for the students to apply their generalization and may suggest other areas of exploration. Students may enjoy forming more exotic polygons and computing their areas as well.

Supplementary Activities: A formula for finding the area of a polygonal region with one or more holes, as in exercise 7, is closely associated with Pick's theorem and students might be encouraged to experiment further to find such a formula. For discussion of this topic see Marshall (1970).

The results of exercise 8 may be used to suggest an investigation into whether for each natural number *n*, one can find a square on dot paper whose area is exactly *n*.

Some students may inquire if Pick's rule can be extended to three dimensions. The answer is yes, but not in the obvious manner. See Niven and Zuckerman (1967).

Answers:

1a. ½, 1, 1½, 2, 2½; 1b. (*c*); 1c. 6½

2a. 2, 2½, 3, 3½; 2b. $A = 1 + \frac{1}{2}b - 1$; 2c. 5

3a. 4, 4½, 5, 5½, 6; 3b. $2 + \frac{1}{2}b - 1 = A$; 3c. 6½

4. $1 + \frac{1}{2}b - 1$, $2 + \frac{1}{2}b - 1$, $3 + \frac{1}{2}b - 1$, $4 + \frac{1}{2}b - 1$, $8 + \frac{1}{2}b - 1$, $i + \frac{1}{2}b - 1$

5a. 1; 5b. 5; 5c. 10; 5d. 12; 5e. 2; 5f. 4

6a. 20½; 6b. 18; 6c. 22

REFERENCES

Harkin, J. B. "The Limit Concept on the Geoboard." Mathematics Teacher 65 (January 1972): 13–17.

Marshall, A. G. "Pick: with Holes." Mathematics Teaching 50 (1970): 67–68.

Niven, I., and H. S. Zuckerman. "Lattice Points and Polygonal Area." *American Mathematical Monthly* 74 (1967): 1195–1200.

Sullivan, John J. "Polygons on a Lattice." Arithmetic Teacher 20 (December 1973): 673–75.

Editorial comment: Pick's theorem is a relatively recent result in elementary Euclidean geometry. It was discovered in 1899 by G. Pick. Note that Pick's theorem implies that the area of any polygonal shape with lattice points as vertices will always be a multiple of 1/2. Many pupils find this surprising. You may find the use of dot paper an interesting setting for introducing the concept of area measure and developing the standard area formulas as well.

DOTS AND AREA

 This polygon has 6 dots on the boundary. We say b = 6. This polygon has 1 dot in the interior. We say i = 1.

1a. Below are some polygons with no dots in the interior (i = 0). Find the area of each of the polygons and record your answers in the table provided. The figure labeled E has an area of 1.

Interior Dots	Boundary Dots	Area
i	b	A
0	3	
0	4	
0	5	
0	6	
0	7	

b. Circle the rule that shows how to find the area when the number of boundary dots (b) is known and the number of interior dots (i) is 0.

   (a) $A = b + 1$ (b) $A = 2b - 2$ (c) $A = \frac{1}{2}b - 1$ (d) $A = b^2 - 2$

c. What do you think the area of a polygon would be if it has exactly 15 dots on its boundary and no dots inside?

d. Form such a polygon and find its area.

2a. The following polygons have 1 dot in the interior. Find the area and enter it in the table.

Interior Dots	Boundary Dots	Area
i	b	A
1	4	
1	5	
1	6	
1	7	

b. When i = 1, write a formula relating b to A.

c. Find the area when b = 10 and i = 1. Draw the polygon and check your result.

3a. Exactly 2 dots are inside each polygon (i = 2) below. The numbers of dots on the boundaries are different.

Find the area of each of these polygons and record your answers in the table provided.

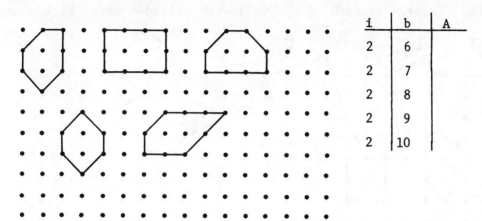

i	b	A
2	6	
2	7	
2	8	
2	9	
2	10	

b. State a rule relating b to A when i = 2 for these polygons.

_____

c. Find the area when b = 11 and i = 2. Draw the polygon and check your result.

4. Using the results of questions 1 to 4 complete the following table. You will have to look for a pattern.

dots inside (i)	0	1	2	3	4	8	i
dots on boundary	b	b	b	b	b	b	b
Area	$0 + \frac{1}{2}b - 1$						

The rule that you discovered, $A = i + \frac{1}{2}b - 1$, relates the area A of a polygon to the number of dots inside the polygon i and the number of dots on its boundary b. It is known as Pick's rule.

5. Find the area of each of the following polygons using Pick's rule.

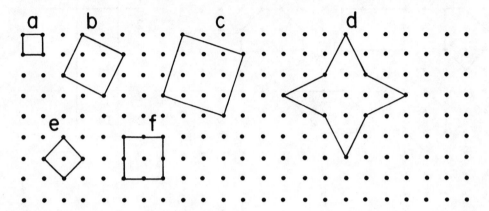

6. Use Pick's rule to find the area of each of the shaded regions.

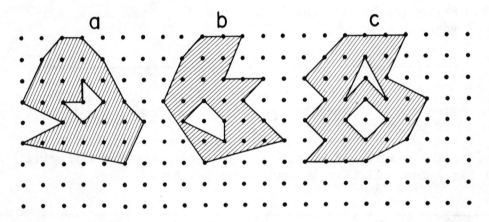

7. Use Pick's rule to help you draw polygons having 3, 4, 5, 6, 7, 8, 9, and 10 sides so that each polygon has the smallest possible area.

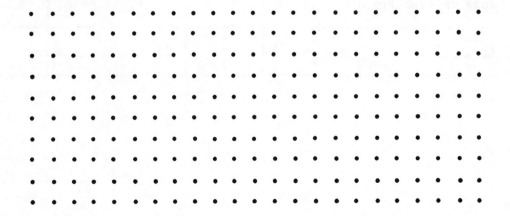

VOLUME AND SURFACE AREA

November 1975

By Gerald Kulm, Purdue University
West Lafayette, Indiana

Teacher's Guide

Grade level: 7–8

Materials: Scissors, cellophane tape, centimeter ruler, sheets 1–3

Objectives: Students will construct open-top rectangular boxes, calculate their volumes and surface areas, and find the most economical box to produce.

Procedure: Make copies of sheets 1–3 and distribute them to students. Students will also need the materials listed above.

You may wish to have groups of three students work together and each construct one of the boxes.

In Part A be sure students understand that each box on sheet 3 is made from a rectangle 10 cm by 7 cm. In Part B some students may find the total surface area by using the formula $2lw + 2wh + lw$. In Part C the amount of material used varies. Thus students must calculate to find which box is most economical.

Answers:

		l	w	h	V
Part A	3–4.				
	Box 1	9 cm	6 cm	.5 cm	27 cm³
	Box 2	8 cm	5 cm	1 cm	40 cm³
	Box 3	6 cm	3 cm	2 cm	36 cm³

5. Box 2

			Box 1	Box 2	Box 3
Part B	6.				
		Area of side	4.5	8	12
		Area of side	4.5	8	12
		Area of end	3.0	5	6
		Area of end	3.0	5	6
		Area of bottom	54	40	18
		T.S.A.	69 cm²	66 cm²	54 cm²

7. Box 3

			Box 1	Box 2	Box 3
Part C	8.				
		Cost/cm³ (in cents)	2.6	1.7	1.5

9. Box 3

Editorial comment: Be sure when using this activity to have your students first estimate which box has the greatest volume and which the greatest surface area. For a more challenging visualization and estimation experience, have them order all three boxes, least to greatest, before doing any computation. Consider also having the students draw a graph plotting the volume against the size of the squares cut out. Three points can be located from the completed tables. To draw an accurate graph they might compute volumes for all possible square sizes, in half-centimeter units, from 0.5 cm to 3 cm. See if any of your students can express the volume in terms of a variable, x, representing the dimension of each square cut from the corners: $V = lwh = (10 — 2x)(7 — 2x)(x)$. Advanced mathematics can be used to show that the maximum volume occurs for a value of x slightly over 1.35 cm.

A cardboard box manufacturer has a flat sheet of cardboard measuring 10 cm x 7 cm. The manufacturer is given an order to form boxes with open tops. This is done by cutting out the corners.

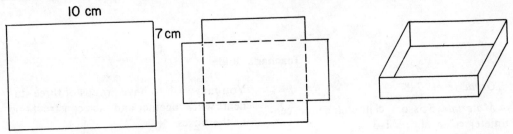

If he cuts larger corners the box will be taller but the base smaller.

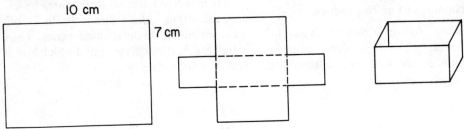

Part A

1. The manufacturer wishes to find the box with the greatest volume. Follow the directions on sheet 3 to form boxes with open tops.

2. Estimate which box has the greatest volume.

3. Measure each box and fill in the first three columns.

	Length (l)	Width (w)	Height (h)	Volume (V)
Box 1	cm	cm	cm	cm^3
Box 2	cm	cm	cm	cm^3
Box 3	cm	cm	cm	cm^3

The volume of the box is the product of the length, the width, and the height. $V = l \cdot w \cdot h$

4. Compute the volume of each box and complete the last column.

5. Which box has the greatest volume?

Part B

The cardboard box manufacturer wants to find the box with the least surface area. The surface area of a box is the sum of the area of its faces.

6. Find the surface area of the 3 boxes.

	Box 1	Box 2	Box 3
Area of side (l · h)			
Area of side (l · h)			
Area of end (w · h)			
Area of end (w · h)			
Area of bottom (l · w)			
Total surface area			

7. Which box has the least surface area?

Part C

The manufacturer finds that he can purchase the boxes already cut out at a cost of 1¢ per square centimeter. He wishes to find the box that is most economical. To find the most economical box he must find the cost per cubic centimeter.

8. Complete the table. Carry answers out to the nearest tenth of a cent.

	Box 1	Box 2	Box 3
$\dfrac{\text{Surface Area} \times \text{Cost Per cm}^2\ (\$0.01)}{\text{Volume}}$			

9. Which box is most economical?

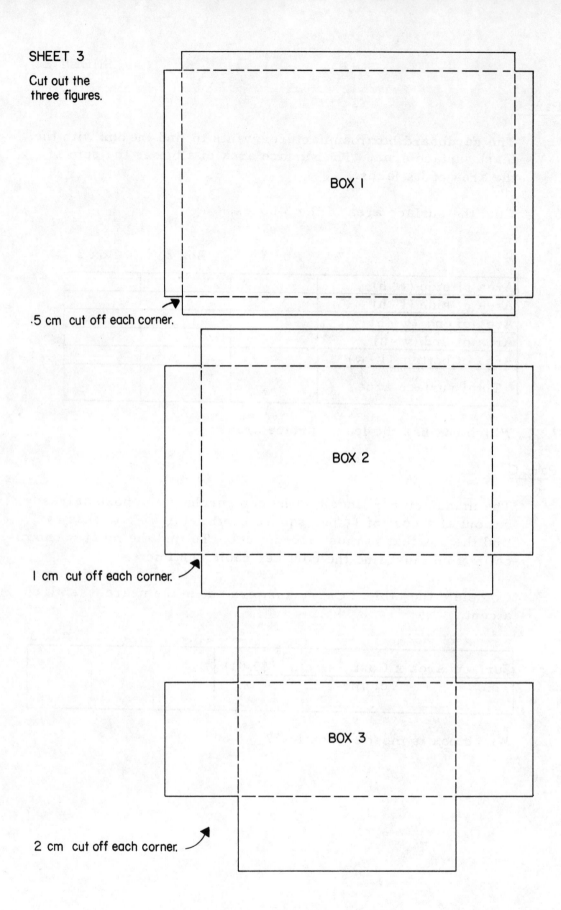

AREA AND COST PER UNIT: AN APPLICATION

April 1980

By Jan J. Vandever, Concordia College, Moorhead, MN 56560

Teacher's Guide

Grade level: 7–10

Materials: One set of worksheets for each student, calculators if available

Objectives: Students will name polygons having four, six, and nine sides. Students will partition some of these regions into simpler polygons to compute areas. Area formulas for a triangle, a square, a rectangle, and a trapezoid will be used to compute the area of the figures so that cost per square unit can be found. Experience is also gained in rounding numbers to the nearest thousandth.

Directions: Make copies of sheets 1–3 and distribute sheets 1 and 2. Use the third worksheet as a separate extension after sheets 1 and 2 have been completed. Calculators may be used for greater accuracy.

Sheets 1 and 2: Students will identify floor shapes and find floor areas for six tents. Each area should be rounded to the nearest square unit before recording. Using the cost figure for each diagram, the student will compute the cost per square unit of floor area. The unit price should be rounded to the nearest tenth of a cent before recording. Some right angles and dimensions are indicated in the figures to help students identify the polygons.

Tent A and Tent B have square and rectangular floors, respectively. Tent C has a trapezoidal floor. Tent D has a hexagonal floor and requires partitioning into two triangles and a trapezoid. In Tent E the three trapezoidal wings are congruent and therefore meet to form an equilateral triangle. The regular hexagonal floor of Tent F can be partitioned into two trapezoids or six equilateral triangles. (Review the use of the Pythagorean theorem in finding the altitude of an equilateral triangle.) Note that if Tent F is partitioned into equilateral triangles with altitudes of 51.1 as given, the floor area will be 9045 square units. However, if the student computes the altitude as $29.5\sqrt{3}$, the floor area will be 9044 square units. Obviously, this difference is due to the rounding error introduced with the 51.1 dimension. Cost per square unit will be the same.

Sheet 3. Sheet 3 contains a brief introduction to the activity and a table to record answers. Students will find the areas of the seven pieces of material that form the tent shown. Shapes are given in the table to help students visualize the figure. Total area of the material and cost per square unit of material will also be computed.

Answers:

Tent	Cost	Shape	Floor Area	Cost per Square Unit of Floor Area
A	$120	square	12 100	0.010
B	$ 98	rectangle	9 030	0.011
C	$195	trapezoid	5 076	0.038
D	$118	hexagon	4 524	0.026
E	$325	nonagon	11 459	0.028
F	$195	regular hexagon	9 045	0.022

The tent that is the least expensive per square unit of floor space is Tent A.

Areas rounded to the nearest square unit for sheet 3 are 2300, 2300, 1272, 1272, 663, 663, and 4600, respectively. The total area of the material required is 13 070, and the cost per square unit of material is 0.015 cents.

Editorial comment: Valuable experiences are gained in doing application activities such as this one. Although the activity deals with measurement, it also requires substantial computational skill, good visualization skill in partitioning the various polygons, and broad problem-solving skill in reading dimensions and breaking down a complex problem into simpler parts. Calculator skills can also be developed. Other similar applications can be prepared that deal with kites, buildings, dress patterns, and the like.

Plans A through F represent the floor plans for six tents. For each plan, name the polygonal shape of the floor and find the floor area, rounded to the nearest square unit. Using the cost figure in the table, compute the cost per square unit of floor area, rounded to the nearest tenth of a cent. Record each answer in the following table.

Tent	Cost	Shape	Floor Area	Cost per Square Unit of Floor Area
A	$120			
B	$ 98			
C	$195			
D	$118			
E	$325			
F	$195			

Which tent is the least expensive per square unit of floor space?_____

PLAN A

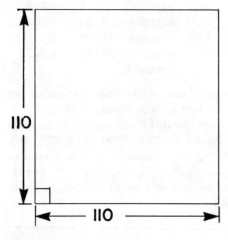

110

110

PLAN B

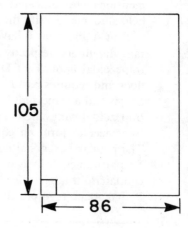

105

86

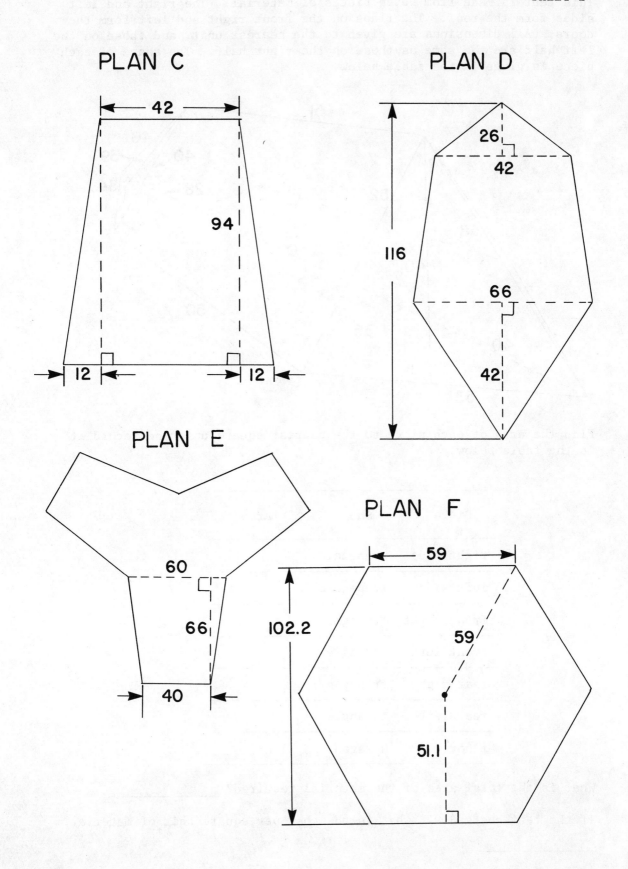

PLAN C

PLAN D

PLAN E

PLAN F

This tent is made from seven pieces of material. The right and left sides form the roof. The flaps on the front right and left form the doors. All dimensions are given to the nearest unit, and those on the left half are the same as those on the right half. The shape of each piece is given in the table below.

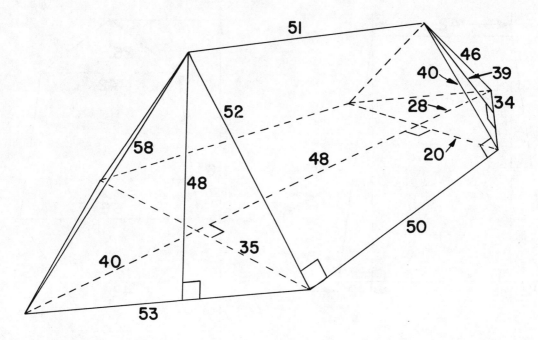

Find the area of each piece to the nearest square unit and record it in the table below.

Piece	Shape	Area
right side	trapezoid	
left side	trapezoid	
front right	triangle	
front left	triangle	
rear right	triangle	
rear left	triangle	
floor	hexagon	

What is the total area of the material required?_____

If the tent costs $197, what is the cost per square unit of material?

_____

Additional Activities for
Measurement

Bolster, L. Carey. "Total Surface Area of Boxes." Oct. 1972, 535–38. Students identify the dimensions of various faces of rectangular boxes drawn in perspective and then compute the area of each face and the total surface area. (Grades 7–8)

Bolster, L. Carey. "Midpoints and Measures." Nov. 1973, 627–30. Pupils find midpoints of given triangles and quadrilaterals using a cutout ruler and then discover relationships involving the measures of the segments connecting these midpoints. (Grades 7–9)

Kullman, David E. "Mission—Measurement." Feb. 1976, 135–38. Students construct a clinometer and a hypsometer and use these instruments together with scale drawings and properties of similar triangles to find the heights of objects. (Grades 7–10)

Watkins, Ann E. "The Isoperimetric Theorem." Feb. 1979, 118–22. Working on square grids, students discover that for a given perimeter, the circle is the closed curve that bounds the greatest area. During this activity they also discover several other relationships between perimeters and areas of simple closed curves. (Grades 7–12)

Activities for
Problem Solving

The National Council of Teachers of Mathematics has recommended that problem solving be the focus of school mathematics in the 1980s. The eight activities in this section provide opportunities for the learner to confront problem situations in a variety of contexts other than the traditional word-problem format. The activities engage students in such problem-solving strategies as organizing data in tables, looking for patterns, first solving simpler related problems, conducting simulations, and generating new solutions from old ones. As your students work through these activities, encourage flexibility and emphasize the methods of solution.

In the lead activity, "Discovery with Cubes," small cubes are stacked to form larger cubes that are then assumed to be submerged in paint. Students are to use spatial visualization to complete a table and thereby discover a pattern that permits them to predict the number of smaller cubes that have 0, 1, 2, 3, or 4 painted faces. "Probability and Pi" introduces the Monte Carlo method for simulating random experiments. Using this method, pupils calculate probabilities and estimates of π by randomly tossing needles and disks onto a square grid and by randomly selecting pairs of numbers from telephone number suffixes.

"Number Triangles—a Discovery Lesson" guides students to discover generalizations regarding Pascal's triangle and triangular arrangements of Fibonacci numbers and integers by organizing data in tables and searching for number patterns. The next activity, "Creativity with Colors," permits students to discover the recently proved four-color theorem and to solve several problems involving the minimum number of colors required to properly color different types of planar maps. In addition, students are encouraged to create their own coloring problems.

In the activity "Isolations" pupils place the consecutive integers 1, 2, 3, . . . , n into designs of n circles so that no two consecutive integers occupy circles connected by a line segment. Reflections, rotations, and complementations are used to generate new solutions from old ones.

"The Vertex Connection" makes explicit the strategy of solving a difficult problem by first solving simpler but related problems. Students discover a formula for the number of diagonals in a convex polygon and then apply their result to solve a real-world problem. They also have an opportunity to play and analyze the related game of SIM.

"Pattern Gazing" focuses on pupils' organizing data in tables, discovering patterns, and then formulating generalizations regarding the sums of series. The final activity, "Polycubes," uses cube puzzles as the setting for problem solving. By making models or drawing sketches on graph paper, students determine the number of tetracubes (solids formed from four cubes joined face to face) and pentacubes that can be formed. They also construct a Soma cube and are provided a technique for making other polycube puzzles.

An annotated bibliography of additional activities for problem solving appears at the end of this section.

DISCOVERY WITH CUBES

By Robert E. Reys, University of Missouri—Columbia, Columbia, Missouri

Teacher's Guide

Grade level: 6–12

Materials: Student worksheets

Objectives: Students will visualize three-dimensional figures, construct a table, discover patterns in the table, and use patterns to make predictions.

Directions: Make copies of the tear-out pages for students. Divide the class into groups of two each, and let them work together to solve this exercise. It would be quite helpful if the teacher had a set of cubes that were colored as stated in activities 1–3. In this way, students could verify their results.

After completing activity 4, students should record their results in the table (activity 6) found on worksheet 3. Check the table with the class to insure that all students have the correct values, since predictions will be made on the basis of their data. Students should then sketch or construct a 6 × 6 × 6 cube as indicated in activity 5 and add its data to the table.

Few students will be able to complete the table for a 10 × 10 × 10 cube unless some patterns have been identified. Ask, "Are there any constants in a column? Any multiples?" Encouraging pupils to keep track of the factors used in the table aids pattern recognition. For example, 0, 6, 24, 54, and 96 are the first five values for one of the columns. A pattern is more discernible when these values are written as 0, 6 × 1, 6 × 4, 6 × 9, and 6 × 16.

Here is a question that might be used to culminate this activity: "Let the length of one side of the cube be N. When you complete this row of the table, is the sum of these values N^3?"

Solutions:

Activity 1: a. 8; b. 8; c. 0; d. 0; e. 0; f. 8; g. equal

Activity 2: a. 27; b. 8; c. 12; d. 6; e. 1; f. 27; g. equal

Activity 3: a. 64; b. 8; c. 24; d. 24; e. 8; f. 64; g. equal

Activity 4: a. 125; b. 8; c. 36; d. 54; e. 27; f. 125; g. equal

---

Editorial comment: Additional answers for the table in Activity 6 include the following:

6 × 6 × 6	64	96	48	8	Total 216
7 × 7 × 7	125	150	60	8	Total 343
10 × 10 × 10	512	384	96	8	Total 1000

Exploring the results for an $n \times n \times n$ cube yields a key discovery:

$n \times n \times n$	$(n-2)^3$	$12(n-2)^2$	$6(n-2)$	8	Total n^3

The coefficients 12, 6, and 8 are the number of edges, faces, and vertices of a cube. These, of course, are the locations of those small cubes with 1, 2, and 3 painted faces, respectively.

Interesting modifications can be made on this activity by changing the painting process. How would the small cubes be painted if only the lateral faces of the large cube were painted? If just the top and bottom faces were painted? If three different colors were used, each on a different pair of opposite faces?

Name_____

DISCOVERY WITH CUBES

Small cubes have been stacked and glued together to form these larger cubes.

Activity 1

    a.   How many small cubes are in the large cube? _____

        If this large cube is dropped into a bucket of paint and completely submerged:

    b.   How many of the smaller cubes are painted on three sides? _____

    c.   How many on only two sides? _____

    d.   How many on only one side? _____

    e.   How many on zero sides? _____

    f.   What is the sum of your answers in b, c, d, and e? _____

    g.   How does your answer to f compare to a? _____

Activity 2

    a.   How many small cubes are in the large cube? _____

    b.   How many of the smaller cubes are painted on three sides? _____

    c.   How many on only two sides? _____

    d.   How many on only one side? _____

    e.   How many on zero sides? _____

    f.   What is the sum of your answers in b, c, d, and e? _____

    g.   How does your answer to f compare to a? _____

SHEET 2

Activity 3

    a. How many small cubes are in this large cube?_____

        If this large cube is dropped into a bucket of paint and completely submerged:

    b. How many of the smaller cubes are painted on three sides? _____

    c. How many on only two sides?_____

    d. How many on only one side?_____

    e. How many on zero sides?_____

    f. What is the sum of your answers in b, c, d, and e?_____

    g. How does your answer to f compare to a?_____

Activity 4

    a. How many small cubes make up this large cube?_____

        If this large cube is dropped into a bucket of paint and completely submerged:

    b. How many of the smaller cubes are painted on three sides?_____

    c. How many on only two sides?_____

    d. How many on only one side?_____

    e. How many on zero sides?_____

    f. What is the sum of your answers in b, c, d, and e?_____

    g. How does your answer to f compare to a? _____

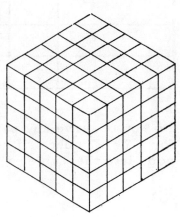

Activity 5

Suppose your cube was 6x6x6. Complete this model by sketching a 6x6x6 cube. Use it to determine the total number of cubes as well as the number of faces with zero, one, two, three and four sides painted.

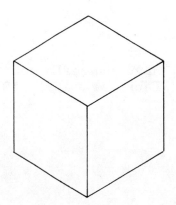

SHEET 3

Activity 6

Now that you have solved several problems with the cubes, record this information in the Table:

Length of Side of Cube	Number of Painted Sides					Total Number of Cubes
	0	1	2	3	4	
2						
3						
4						
5						
6						

Do you observe any patterns? _____ If so, complete the Table for a 7x7x7 cube. If not, sketch or construct a cube and then complete the Table.

Have you really got the idea? If you think so, try to complete the Table for a 10x10x10 cube.

PROBABILITY AND PI

September 1977

By Christian R. Hirsch, Western Michigan University, Kalamazoo, MI 49008

Teacher's Guide

Grade level: 7–12

Materials: Wire (coat hangers) or thin strips of wood, cutters, tagboard, compasses, scissors, phone book, and copies of sheets 1–3

Objectives: Students are to calculate estimates of π using Monte Carlo techniques and compare the relative accuracy of their approximations.

Procedure: Distribute worksheets to each student. Note that sheets 1 and 2 can also be completed using a checkerboard, with a corresponding scaling down of the other apparatus. In particular, for squares of length l, use a needle of length l and a saucer with radius $\frac{1}{4} l$.

You may wish to have students work on this activity in pairs. In this way, sheets 1 and 2 can be completed by having one pupil perform the indicated experiment while the other records the successes. On sheet 3 each student can check on the other's calculations. These experimental results can then be pooled to obtain a much larger sample, which should yield closer approximations for π and on which comparisons can be based.

The second experiment is amenable to further analysis, and some students might be encouraged to discover the mathematical rationale behind the probability formula. This can be done by a comparison of areas. Assume that the center of the saucer lands anywhere in a given square. The saucer will touch a vertex, provided its center is in one of the four quarter circles of the

same radius centered at each vertex. Comparing this total area to the area of the square yields $\pi/16$.

The mathematics underlying the probability formulas on sheets 1 and 3 is beyond the scope of most secondary school students. However, completion of the third experiment will produce some very fruitful mathematical discussions. For example, how does one determine if two numbers are relatively prime? One possible way is to compare their prime factorizations, if simple divisibility tests are not productive. Is there an easier way? The Euclidean algorithm, illustrated below, is a particularly efficient technique for finding the greatest common factor (gcf) of pairs of large numbers.

To find the gcf of 840 and 329, proceed as follows:

$$840 = 329(2) + 182$$
$$329 = 182(1) + 147$$
$$182 = 147(1) + 35$$
$$147 = 35(4) + 7$$
$$35 = 7(5) + 0$$

The last nonzero remainder, which in this case is 7, will be the gcf. Hence, 840 and 329 are *not* relatively prime.

REFERENCES

Ogilvy, C. S., and J. T. Anderson. *Excursions in Number Theory.* New York: Oxford University Press, 1966.

Schaaf, W. L. *Nature and History of π.* Stanford, Calif.: School Mathematics Study Group, 1967.

Editorial comment: The Monte Carlo method illustrated in this activity is an important problem-solving technique to which most students should be introduced. It permits students with relatively little mathematical background to obtain estimates of solutions for nontrivial probability and expected-value problems. As an example of the latter application, you might pose the following problem. Suppose a cereal manufacturer includes a felt-tipped pen of one of six different colors in each box. How many boxes of cereal would you expect to buy to get a complete set? Associate each number on a die with a pen color and roll the die until you have a pen of each color. Repeating this simulation several times and then finding the average number of boxes purchased will provide an estimate of the solution. Increasing the number of trials will improve the estimate. An elaboration of this problem can be found in the chapter by Kenneth J. Travers in NCTM's 1981 Yearbook, *Teaching Statistics and Probability.*

Tossing Needles

You probably first encountered the number π in your study of geometry. You learned that π is the ratio of the circumference of a circle to its diameter (C/d). This number, however, has many other interesting properties, some of which you will use in this activity to obtain decimal approximations of the value of π.

1. Observe your classroom floor. It is probably covered with square tiles.

2. From a piece of wire or a thin strip of wood, cut a needle the same length as a side of the square tile.

3. If you toss this needle up in the air, what is the probability that it will fall completely within one of the squares?

    a. One way of estimating this probability is to actually toss the needle 100 times and record the number(s) of successes--that is, how many times the needle falls completely within one of the squares.

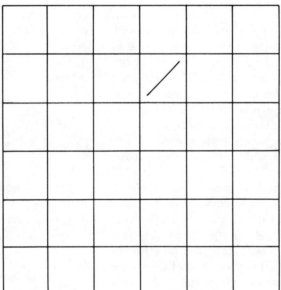

    Calculate s/100 to estimate this probability: _____

    b. This value is also an estimate of π − 3.

    What would be your estimate of π ? _____

4. Let n be the total number of needle tosses in your class and let t equal the total number of successful tosses. Find a class estimate for π by computing t/n + 3: _____

Tossing Saucers

Here is another simple experiment for finding an estimate of π by using probability.

1. From a piece of tagboard, cut a circular saucer having a radius one quarter the length of a side of the square floor tile.

2. If you toss this saucer up in the air, what is the probability that it will land touching a vertex of one of the square floor tiles?

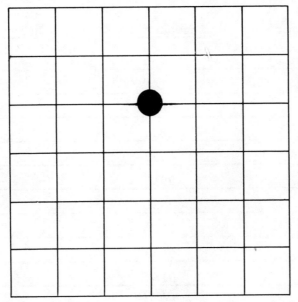

a. Perform this experiment 100 times and record the number(s) of successes. Then compute the probability estimate, s/100:

    _____

b. The value above is also an estimate of π/16.

    What would be your estimate of π this time? _____

3. Let n be the total number of saucer tosses in your class and let t be the total number of times the saucer touched a vertex of a square.

    Determine a class estimate for π: _____

Searching Phone Books

1. Recall that two positive integers are said to be relatively prime if they have no common factor other than 1. For example, 8 and 9 are relatively prime.

   If two numbers are written down at random, what is the probability that they will be relatively prime?

2. Let's actually perform the experiment. Below are ten pairs of numbers selected at random from telephone number suffixes.

First number	Second number	Relatively prime?
0762	3804	No
6006	0181	
3871	6622	
4129	2830	
1294	4257	
0585	9916	
8663	2531	
2890	8310	
9148	5433	
1620	0185	

   a. Determine which of these pairs of numbers are relatively prime.

   b. Randomly select ten more pairs of numbers from telephone number suffixes in a local phone book and determine which of these pairs of numbers are relatively prime.

   c. Let s equal the number of pairs that were relatively prime.

      Calculate the probability estimate s/20: _____

   d. This value is also an estimate of $6/\pi^2$.

      Use your answer in part c to determine an estimate for
      π: _____

3. Pool your results with those of other classmates to determine a class approximation for π: _____

4. The value of π correct to 5 decimal places is 3.14159. Which of the three experiments yielded the closest class approximation?

NUMBER TRIANGLES—A DISCOVERY LESSON

December 1975

By Hugh Ouellette, Winona State College, Winona, Minnesota

Teacher's Guide

Grade level: 7–12

Materials: Student worksheets and scratch paper; transparencies for classroom demonstration and discussion

Objectives: Students will experience the inductive problem-solving techniques of collecting data by working simple but related problems, organizing and acquiring data, searching for patterns, and forming generalizations based on discovered patterns.

Directions: Distribute the worksheets one at a time. Have the students work either individually or in small groups of two or three. After completing sheet 1, have the students discuss their answers and their discoveries. Then develop a complete set of answers on the transparency. Repeat the same procedure for sheets 2 and 3.

Comments: As the students work on the exercises, circulate among them. Stress that all computations should be accurate and predictions checked. Be receptive to partial solutions and incomplete reasoning patterns. Emphasize that any generalizations made have not been proved. However, it should be noted that the activities provide a wealth of exercises to which the technique of mathematical induction can be developed and applied.

Supplementary Problems:

Sheet 1

1. In row 100, what is the 5th term? the 190th term?
2. What is the mean of all terms in row 100?

3. Find the sum of all terms in the first 18 rows.

Sheet 2

1. The numeral 10 011 is in row 100. In the next row, what numeral is directly below and to the left of it?
2. Find the sum of the first 20 rows.

Sheet 3

1. What are the first and second terms in row 1812?
2. The sum of the terms in diagonal 2 (1, 3, 6, 10, ...) down to row 100 will be found at the intersection of what row and diagonal?

Answers:

Sheet 1

2. 1, 2, 3, 4, 5, 6, 7; 100
3. 1, 3, 5, 7, 9, 11, 13; 199
4. 1, 4, 9, 16, 25, 36, 49; 10 000
5. For square $\begin{array}{|c|c|}\hline A & B \\\hline C & D \\\hline\end{array}$

$A + D = B + C$; $|AD - BC| = 1$; $A + B = C + D - 2$; $|(A + C) - (B + D)| = 2$

Sheet 2

2. 1, 2, 3, 4, 5, 6, 7; 100
3. 1, 4, 9, 16, 25, 36, 49; 10 000
4. 1, 3, 7, 13, 21, 31, 43; 9901
5. 1, 8, 27, 64, 125, 216, 343; 1 000 000 (100^3)

Sheet 3

1. 1 6 15 20 15 6 1
   1 7 21 35 35 21 7 1
2. 2, 4, 8, 16, 32, 64, 128; 2^{100} (approximately 1.27×10^{30})
3. 3, 7, 15, 31, 63, 127, 255; $2^{101} - 1$
4. all 0's

Editorial comment: Pattern recognition is a very powerful tool in many problem-solving situations. This activity offers extensive opportunity to practice this skill. For some, the patterns will be easy to recognize. For others, careful step-by-step directions and helpful hints will be necessary before they make any discoveries. In both cases, allow sufficient time for students' own explorations and encourage the discussion of their "discoveries," whether correct or otherwise. Similar exploration of number patterns can be made using other arrays such as the addition and multiplication tables or the monthly calendar.

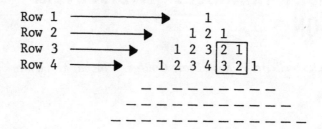

1. Study the INTEGER TRIANGLE shown. Then extend it to three more rows.

2. Find the MIDDLE TERM for each of the first seven rows. Then predict
    the middle term for row 100.

Row number	1	2	3	4	5	6	7	...	100
Middle term									

3. Find the NUMBER OF TERMS for each of the first seven rows. Then pre-
    dict the number of terms for row 100.

Row number	1	2	3	4	5	6	7	...	100
Number of terms									

4. Find the SUM of the terms for each of the first seven rows. Then pre-
    dict the sum for row 100.

Row number	1	2	3	4	5	6	7	...	100
Sum									

5. A four-number square has been outlined in the triangle. The sums of
    both pairs of opposite corner numbers is 4.

$$2 + 2 = 4 \qquad\qquad 1 + 3 = 4$$

The products of these opposite pairs of numbers are 4 and 3.

$$2 \times 2 = 4 \qquad\qquad 1 \times 3 = 3$$

Find these sums and products for several more four-number squares.
Then state two relationships that appear always to exist for such
squares.

```
Row 1  ──────────▶  1
Row 2  ─────────▶   3   5
Row 3  ────────▶   7   9   11
Row 4  ──────▶  13  15  17  19
Row 5  ───▶  21  23  25  27  29
           ─   ─   ─   ─   ─   ─
         ─   ─   ─   ─   ─   ─   ─
```

1. Study the part of FIBONACCI'S TRIANGLE shown.
   Then extend it two more rows.

2. Find the NUMBER OF TERMS for each of the first seven rows.
   Then predict the number of terms in row 100.

Row number	1	2	3	4	5	6	7	...	100
Number of terms									

3. The MEAN or average of the <u>first</u> and <u>last</u> terms in row 4 is
   (13 + 19)/2, which is 16. Find these means for each of the first
   seven rows. Then predict the mean for row 100.

Row number	1	2	3	4	5	6	7	...	100
Mean of first and last term				16					

4. The FIRST TERM in row 3 is (2 x 3) + 1 = 7.
   The first term in row 4 is (3 x 4) + 1 = 13.
   The first term in row 5 is (4 x 5) + 1 = 21.
   See if the first terms in the other rows can be found the same way.
   Then predict the first term for row 100.

Row number	1	2	3	4	5	6	7	...	100
First term			7	13	21				

5. The SUM of the numbers in row 4 is $13 + 15 + 17 + 19 = 64 = 4^3$.
   Find the sums of the numbers in the other rows.
   Next represent each sum using exponents.
   Then predict the sum for row 100.

Row number	1	2	3	4	5	6	7	...	100
Sum				64					
Sum, using exponents				4^3					

Activities from the *Mathematics Teacher*   117

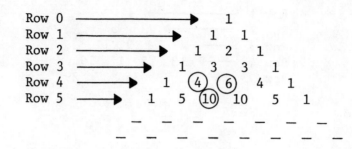

1. Study the part of PASCAL'S TRIANGLE shown. Each row begins and ends with 1. Every other term equals the sum of the two numbers directly above to the left and right. The circled 10 is the sum of the circled 4 and 6. Check this relationship for other entries, and then extend the triangle for two more rows.

2. The SUM of the terms in row 3 is 8. Eight can be expressed as 2^3. Find the sum of the terms in each of the first seven rows. Next represent each sum using exponents, and then predict the sum for row 100.

Row number	1	2	3	4	5	6	7	...	100
Sum			8						
Sum, using exponents			2^3						

3. The SUM OF ALL TERMS through row 2 is 7: $1+(1+1)+(1+2+1) = 7$
    The number 7 is 1 less than 8, which can
                        be written $2^3 - 1 = 7.$
    The sum of all terms through row 3 is $2^4 - 1 = 15.$
    The sum of all terms through row 4 is $2^5 - 1 = 31.$
    Work similar problems to check the sums for the other rows.
    Then predict the sum of all terms through row 100.

Row number	1	2	3	4	5	6	7	...	100
Sum through this row		7	15	31					

4. ALTERNATELY SUBTRACTING AND ADDING TERMS in row 4 gives 0.

                        $1 - 4 + 6 - 4 + 1 = 0$

    Do the same for the rest of the first seven rows.
    Then predict the results for row 100.

Row number	1	2	3	4	5	6	7	...	100
Alternately subtracting and adding terms				0					

CREATIVITY WITH COLORS

March 1976

By Christian R. Hirsch, Western Michigan University, Kalamazoo, Michigan 49001

Teacher's Guide

Grade level: 7–12

Materials: Colored pencils, one set of worksheets for each student, and a set of transparencies for class discussion

Objective: Students will discover the minimum number of colors required to properly color various types of planar maps.

Directions: It may be preferable to have students complete this activity working in small groups. Colored pencils can then be distributed to each group and a set of worksheets to each student. Note that regions that are to be the same color can be numbered with the same number, though many pupils find this method less enjoyable than coloring.

Sheet 1: Students should have little difficulty discovering that maps (a)–(f) can be properly colored using 3, 3, 4, 3, 2, and 4 colors, respectively.

Sheet 2: In this activity students should be required to form several maps of each type before generalizing. Maps formed as in questions 2 and 4 can always be properly colored using only two colors. Problem 6 requires three colors.

Pupils who have had some work with mathematical induction may wish to try proving their generalizations. Others might be encouraged to create their own coloring problems (e.g., How many colors are needed to properly color various tessellations? What would happen if, in question 4, circles were replaced by polygons such as rectangles?).

Sheet 3: Students color actual maps using the least number of colors possible. All maps in problem 7 require the use of four colors. Question 8 leads up to the famous four-color conjecture. Though it has been proved that no more than five colors are needed, it is conjectured that four are sufficient. A brief historical account and proof of the five-color theorem may be found in Ore (1963).

REFERENCES

Dynkin, E., and V. Uspenskii. *Mathematical Conversations, Part I: Multicolor Problems.* Translated by N. Whaland, Jr. and R. Brown. Boston: D. C. Heath & Co., 1963.

Ore, Oystein. *Graphs and Their Uses.* New York: Random House, 1963.

Editorial comment: A proof of the four-color conjecture was completed in June 1976 by two mathematicians, Kenneth Appel and Wolfgang Haken, at the University of Illinois. Their proof required 1200 hours of computer time. In fact, its correctness cannot be checked without the use of a computer. A nontechnical description of their method of proof can be found in *Scientific American* (October 1977).

CREATIVITY WITH COLORS

Most maps are made so that countries or states next to each other are different colors. Maps are colored so that

    a. No two regions with a common boundary have the same color.

    b. Regions that meet only at 1 point can be the same color.

1.   Color these maps using the rules above. Color the complete region inside the rectangle. Use the fewest colors possible.

a.

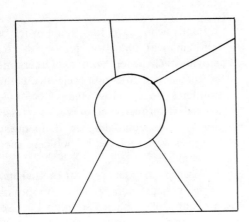

b.

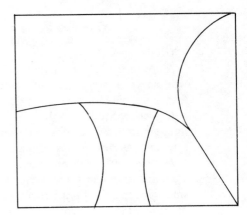

c.

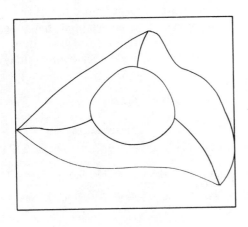

d.

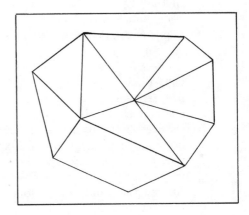

e.

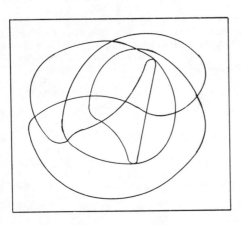

f.

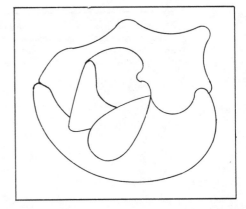

2. Suppose a map is formed by drawing any number of straight lines in the plane. Color the maps as before.

a.
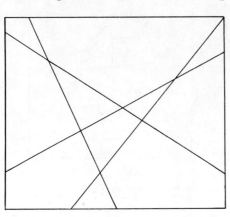

b.
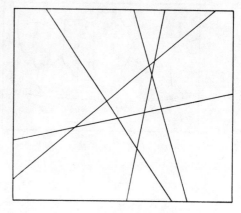

3. Draw several more maps and determine the least number of colors needed for maps of this type.

4. These maps are formed by drawing any number of circles in the plane. Color the maps as before.

a.
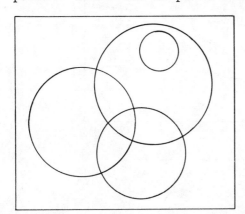

b.
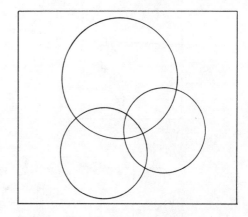

5. Draw several more maps and determine the least number of colors necessary to color maps formed in this way.

6. These maps are formed by drawing circles and then, in each circle a chord is drawn such that chords of two different circles have at most one point in common. How many colors are needed to color these maps?

a.
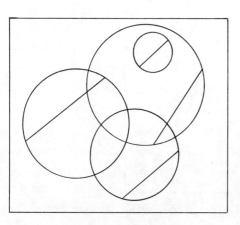

b.
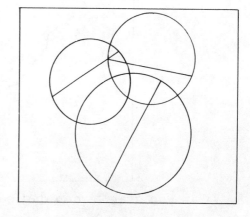

7.   Color these maps.   Use the least amount of colors possible.

a.

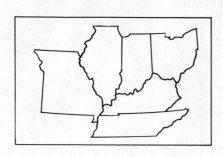

b.

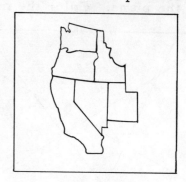

c.

d.

8.   Can you draw a map that cannot be colored with fewer than five colors?

ISOLATIONS

By Donald T. Piele, The University of Wisconsin—Parkside
Kenosha, Wisconsin

Teacher's Guide

Grade level: 7–12

Materials: Activity sheets for each student

Objectives: To investigate simple combinatorial problems and develop strategies for counting the number of distinct solutions

Directions: Each design presents a challenge: Can you place the consecutive integers $(1, 2, 3, \ldots, n)$ into the n circles so that each integer becomes isolated? Isolation occurs when no two consecutive integers occupy circles connected together by a line.

Discussion: For the simple four-in-a-row design, 2-4-1-3 and 3-1-4-2 are solutions, but 1-3-4-2 is clearly not a solution (3 and 4 remain connected). Each solution is called an *isolation* because the consecutive integers are now completely isolated in the design and enjoy a new set of neighbors.

In the beginning, solutions are best discovered by trial and error. Students are challenged just to find one solution for some designs. However, as students exchange their discoveries with one another the question naturally arises:

For a given design, how many isolation solutions are there?

Some hints for generating new solutions from old ones are discussed on sheet 2. The terms *reflection, rotation,* and *complement,* encountered in geometry and modular arithmetic, are defined and used for this purpose. Watch out though—newly generated solutions must be constantly checked to verify that they are indeed new.

Suggestions:

1. Additional investigations can be launched with the following questions:

a. For each design many reflections are possible. Which reflections produce new solutions? Consider the same question about rotations.

b. Find designs that have the same reflection as complement; the same rotation as complement; the same rotation and reflection as complement.

2. Mirrors, transparencies, and the overhead projector are helpful teaching aids to use.

3. Display the solutions on a bulletin board.

Solutions: Five-in-a-row, 14; pentagon, 10; diamond, 0; orange crate, 24; cross, 36; beehive, 60; pyramid, 28; kite, 4.

Editorial comment: The major goal in this activity is one of exploration. As suggested in the teacher's guide, students need a great deal of experience in developing strategies that can be used to find solutions related to those that first emerge from a trial-and-error process. Take the class time necessary for students to discuss their own ways of attacking the problems.

Place the integers 1, 2, 3, and 4 in the circles so that no two connected circles contain consecutive integers. See how many you can complete.

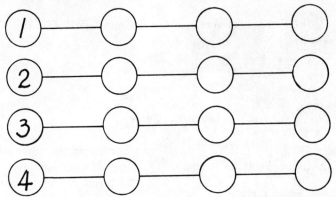

With four circles connected in a row, only two solutions are possible. One sequence starts with 2 and the other with 3. Furthermore, one solution is the reverse of the other. Did you find them both?

Solutions to designs of this type are called <u>isolations,</u> since they isolate the consecutive integers from one another. Each design below has five circles so that no two connected circles contain consecutive integers. Find as many isolation solutions as you can for each design.

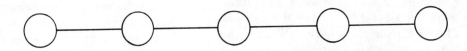

Five-in-a-row

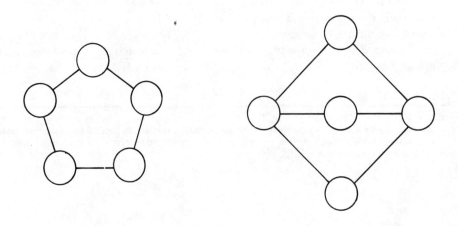

Pentagon   Diamond

How can you find isolation solutions to a given design? Several methods
are possible. One approach starts by finding all possible solutions with
a given number in a given position.

Here are three solutions to the "orange crate" design. These are the only
ones possible with a 1 in the upper left circle.

Row 1
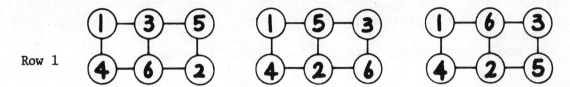

If a mirror is placed above each of the orange crate designs in row 1, the
reflections are also orange crate designs. However, different reflected
solutions are formed. Study how the first has been formed and complete
the rest by similar reflections.

Row 2
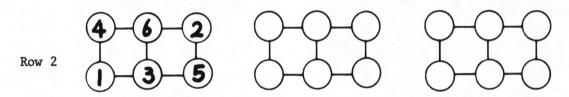

If the orange crate designs in row 1 are rotated 180°, more orange crate
designs result. However, different rotated solutions are formed. Again,
study the first and complete the rest by similar rotations.

Row 3
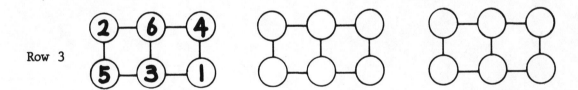

Each solution also has a complement. To find it, subtract each integer
from one more than the number of circles in the design. For the orange
crate design, subtract each number from 7. Complete the complements of
the solutions in row 1.

Row 4
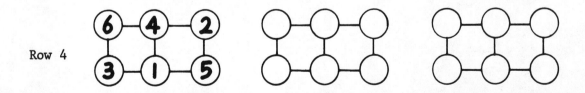

Are all these complements new solutions? Try complementing, reflecting,
and rotating solutions from other rows to find other new solutions.
Search for some where 1 is not in the corner. All told, there are 24
isolation solutions to the orange crate design. How many can you find?

Try your skill with these designs.

1. Find as many isolation solutions as possible.
2. Use the same number of integers as there are circles.
3. Remember, consecutive integers must not be connected together by a line.
4. Use reflections, rotations, and complementations to check for new solutions.
5. Test some of your own strategies for finding solutions.

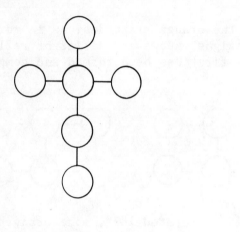

Cross

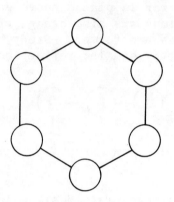

Beehive

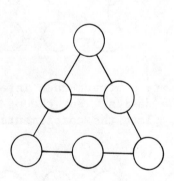

Pyramid

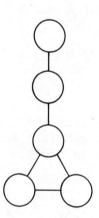

Kite

Make up some designs of your own.

Solve them yourself.

Then give them to classmates to try.

THE VERTEX CONNECTION

November 1976

By Christian R. Hirsch, Western Michigan University, Kalamazoo, MI 49001

Teacher's Guide

Grade level: 7–12

Materials: One set of worksheets for each student and a set of transparencies for classroom discussion if desired

Objectives: Students will (1) discover and apply the formula for the number of diagonals in a polygon and (2) play and analyze the game of SIM.

Directions: Distribute the worksheets one at a time.

Sheet 1: Most students should have little difficulty discovering that the number of diagonals in an *n*-gon is $n(n-3)/2$. However, some may require additional guidance to detect the pattern in the table. Note that this formula was based on an analysis of convex polygons. Students might be encouraged to investigate if their formula also holds for polygons that are not convex.

Sheet 2: In this activity, students are placed in a problem-solving situation that can be modeled using polygons. If class members are represented by the vertices of an *n*-gon, then the number of handshakes involved is equivalent to the number of sides of the polygon formed plus the number of diagonals, $n + n(n-3)/2 = n(n-1)/2$.

Students who have had some work with mathematical induction may wish to try proving this generalization and the one regarding the number of diagonals of an *n*-gon. Others might explore related questions

such as these: How many triangles result if all diagonals from one vertex of an *n*-gon are drawn? What is the maximum number of lines determined by *n* points in the same plane?

Sheet 3: The game of SIM (Simmons 1969) is a two-person game that is handled most effectively by declaring the one who wins two out of three games the winner and then pairing the winners against each other until a class champion emerges. The results of this tournament will suggest that the game always has a winner and that the second player has a better chance of winning. An analysis of a winning strategy may be found in Mead, Rosa, and Huang (1974). The fact that there is always formed a triangle of one of the two colors guarantees an affirmative answer to problem 8. This fact can be easily proved as in Harary (1972). When SIM is played on five vertices, there need not always be a winner.

REFERENCES

Harary, F. "The Two-Triangle Case of the Acquaintance Graph." *Mathematics Magazine* 45 (May 1972): 130–35.

Mead, E., S. Rosa, and C. Huang. "The Game of SIM: A Winning Strategy for the Second Player." *Mathematics Magazine* 47 (November 1974): 243–47.

Simmons, G. "The Game of SIM." *Journal of Recreational Mathematics* 2 (April 1969): 66.

Editorial comment: Sheet 2 illustrates nicely the process of forming a mathematical model for a real-world problem. This same model can be used to solve many related but physically different situations. To illustrate this you might pose the following problem. Suppose the plans for a new office complex call for fifty-two offices equipped with intercoms that will provide for connections between each pair of terminals. How many communication lines will be required?

A <u>diagonal</u> of a polygon is a line segment connecting two vertices that are not endpoints of the same side.

1. Determine the number of diagonals in each of the polygons below and enter your answers in the following table:

Polygon	Number of vertices	Number of diagonals from each vertex	Total number of diagonals
Triangle			
Quadrilateral			
Pentagon			
Hexagon			
Heptagon			
Octagon			

Triangle   Quadrilateral   Pentagon

Hexagon   Heptagon   Octagon

2. a. How many diagonals do you think a polygon with ten sides would have? (Hint: Do you see any pattern in the table above?)

   b. Draw such a polygon and verify your answer.

3. How many diagonals has a polygon with n sides?

4. Suppose at the end of your class today, each student present shakes hands just once with every other student. How many handshakes would be involved?

   Hint: First consider some simpler problems:

   a. Suppose that there are only four members present.

      Represent each member by a vertex of a quadrilateral.

      Indicate all possible handshakes by connecting the appropriate vertices.

      How many handshakes are involved?

   b. Use the method above to determine the number of handshakes if seven students are present.

   c. Do you see any relationship between these solutions and your work on SHEET 1?

   d. Now try to answer the original problem which was posed.

5. How many handshakes would be involved if a class consisted of n members?

6. Here is an interesting game involving vertex connections which you can play with a friend.

    a. Place six points on a sheet of paper to mark the vertices of a regular hexagon as in Figure A below.

    b. Each player selects a color different from the other.

    c. Take turns connecting pairs of points with line segments. (See Figure B for a partially completed game.)

    d. The first player who is forced to form a triangle of his own color is the loser! (Only triangles whose vertices are among the six starting points count.)

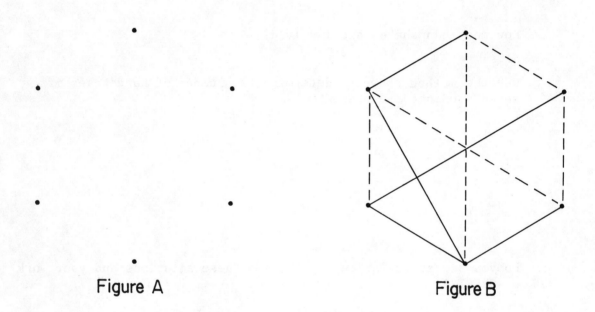

Figure A   Figure B

7. Play this game several times and then answer the questions below.

    a. Is there always a winner?

    b. Which player has the better chance of winning?

8. Use the results of question 7 (a) to help you solve the following problem.

    Of any six students in a room, must there be at least three mutual acquaintances or at least three mutual strangers?

9. Play several more games, but in each case starting with five points that are the vertices of a regular pentagon, and then answer questions 7 (a) and 7 (b).

130   Activities from the *Mathematics Teacher*

PATTERN GAZING

January 1979

By Cherie Adler Aviv, University of Georgia, Athens, GA 30602

Teacher's Guide

Grade Levels: 7–12

Materials: One set of worksheets for each student, a transparency of each worksheet, calculators (optional)

Objectives: To enable the students to discover patterns and make generalizations

Directions: Distribute the activity sheets one at a time. With each sheet, discuss with the students the information presented in the charts. Be sure they understand that the three dots (. . .) represent unspecified intermediate addends. You may need to discuss how to determine the number of addends N without counting each term. Ask the students to examine the relationship between the last number in the series and N of that series. After the students have completed the tables, encourage them to seek a relationship between N and the sum S. The two series following the table are given to test the student's ability to apply the generalization.

Your students may experience some difficulty in determining N for the first three activities. If so, consider discussing the relationship between the number of terms in the given series with the number of terms in the series of counting numbers. For example, compare the number of terms in the series $1 + 3 + 5$ with $1 + 2 + 3 + 4 + 5 + 6$. Students should recognize that the second series has six terms and can be regrouped as $(1 + 3 + 5) + (2 + 4 + 6)$. Since there are as many odd-number terms as even-number terms, the number of odd-number terms will always be half the number of the terms in the second series. Additional examples of this type may be necessary. This generalization will prove helpful in determining the sum of the series following each table.

After each table, the students are asked to write their rule in words or symbols. For most students, a statement such as "multiply N times itself" for (1) or "multiply N times $(N + 1)$" for (3) should suffice. Ad-

vanced algebra students, however, might be expected to generalize in (3), for example, that $2 + 4 + 6 + \cdots + (2n) = n(n + 1)$.

After the students have completed all the tables, ask them to look back at their results. Encourage the students to see how their rules for the various tables relate to each other. In activity 4, the rule is

$$S = \frac{N(N + 1)}{2}.$$

The rule for activity 6 is $S = \left[\dfrac{N(N + 1)}{2}\right]^2.$

This latter result says that the sum of the first N cubes is the square of the sum of the first N natural numbers.

Most students should be able to substantiate the relationship between charts 3 and 4. In chart 3, $2 + 4 + 6 + \cdots + (2n) = n(n + 1)$, and in chart 4, $1 + 2 + 3 + \cdots + n = n(n + 1)/2$. A statement such as "each term in the series in chart 4 is half the corresponding term in the parallel series in chart 3" should suffice. Students familiar with factoring may see the relationship as $2 + 4 + 6 + \cdots + (2n) = 2(1 + 2 + 3 + \cdots + n)$.

Follow-up Activities: Examine these series for similar patterns: (1) $2 - 4 + 6 - 8 + \cdots$ (2) $1 - 2 + 3 - 4 + \cdots$ (3) $1^2 + 2^2 + 3^2 + \cdots$

Answers:

1. $10^2 = 100$; $13^2 = 169$; $S = N^2$

2. -10; -22; $S = \begin{cases} N \text{ if } N \text{ is odd} \\ -N \text{ if } N \text{ is even} \end{cases}$

3. $(14)(15) = 210$; $(25)(26) = 650$; $S = N(N + 1)$

4. $\dfrac{(18)(19)}{2} = 171$; $\dfrac{(44)(45)}{2} = 990$; $S = \dfrac{N(N + 1)}{2}$

5. -171; 325; $S = \begin{cases} N(N + 1)/2 \text{ if } N \text{ is odd} \\ -N(N + 1)/2 \text{ if } N \text{ is even} \end{cases}$

6. $\left[\dfrac{(14)(15)}{2}\right]^2 = 11025$;

$\left[\dfrac{(20)(21)}{2}\right]^2 = 44100$; $S = \left[\dfrac{N(N + 1)}{2}\right]^2$

Editorial comment: In this activity, the discovery of patterns in numbers is used to make conjectures about their sums and to test the apparent resulting generalizations. Of special value are the sum of the first n odd numbers (Activity 1) and the sum of the first n counting numbers (Activity 4). It is interesting to note and discuss the relationship between the sum of the first n numbers $\dfrac{n(n + 1)}{2}$ and the sum of their cubes $\left[\dfrac{n(n + 1)}{2}\right]^2$.

PATTERN GAZING

(1) Complete this table to see what happens when we add odd numbers.

Series	No. of Addends (N)	Sum (S)
1	1	1
1 + 3	2	4
1 + 3 + 5		
1 + 3 + 5 + 7		
1 + 3 + 5 + 7 + 9		
1 + 3 + 5 + 7 + 9 + 11		

Can you find a way to calculate the sum without adding each

term? If so, use your rule to calculate these sums:

1 + 3 + ··· + 17 + 19 = _____

1 + 3 + ··· + 23 + 25 = _____

Write your rule in words or symbols._____

_____

(2) Let's see what happens when we alternately add and subtract odd

numbers. Complete the table.

Series	No. of Addends (N)	Sum (S)
1	1	1
1 - 3	2	-2
1 - 3 + 5		
1 - 3 + 5 - 7		
1 - 3 + 5 - 7 + 9		

Can you find a way to calculate the sum without alternately

adding and subtracting each term? If so, use your rule to

calculate these sums:

1 - 3 + ··· + 17 - 19 = _____

1 - 3 + ··· + 41 - 43 = _____

Write your rule in words or symbols._____

_____

_____

PATTERN GAZING

(3) Let's try adding even numbers.

Series	No. of Addends (N)	Sum (S)
2	1	2
2 + 4	2	6
2 + 4 + 6		
2 + 4 + 6 + 8		
2 + 4 + 6 + 8 + 10		
2 + 4 + 6 + 8 + 10 + 12		

Can you find a way to calculate the sum without adding each

term? If so, use your rule to calculate these sums:

2 + 4 + 6 + ··· + 26 + 28 = _____

2 + 4 + 6 + ··· + 48 + 50 = _____

Write your rule in words or symbols. _____

_____

(4). Let's see what happens when we add both odd and even numbers.

Series	No. of Addends (N)	Sum (S)
1	1	1
1 + 2	2	3
1 + 2 + 3		
1 + 2 + 3 + 4		
1 + 2 + 3 + 4 + 5		

Can you find a way to calculate the sum without adding each

term? (Hint: Compare chart 4 with chart 3.)

If so, use your rule to calculate these sums:

1 + 2 + ··· + 17 + 18 = _____

1 + 2 + ··· + 43 + 44 = _____

Write your rule in words or symbols. _____

_____

_____

(5) Let's see what happens when we square first and then alternately add and subtract.

Series	No. of Addends (N)	Sum (S)
1^2	1	1
$1^2 - 2^2$	2	-3
$1^2 - 2^2 + 3^2$		
$1^2 - 2^2 + 3^2 - 4^2$		
$1^2 - 2^2 + 3^2 - 4^2 + 5^2$		

Can you find a way to calculate the sum without alternately adding and subtracting each term? (HINT: Compare chart 5 with chart 4.)

If so, use your rule to calculate these sums:

$1^2 - 2^2 + \cdots + 17^2 - 18^2 = $ _____

$1^2 - 2^2 + \cdots - 24^2 + 25^2 = $ _____

Write your rule in words or symbols. _____

_____

(6) What about adding the cubes of the counting numbers? Complete the table.

Series	No. of Addends (N)	Sum (S)
1^3	1	1
$1^3 + 2^3$	2	9
$1^3 + 2^3 + 3^3$		
$1^3 + 2^3 + 3^3 + 4^3$		
$1^3 + 2^3 + 3^3 + 4^3 + 5^3$		

Can you find a way to calculate the sum without adding each term?

(HINT: Compare chart 6 with chart 4.)

If so, use your rule to calculate these sums:

$1^3 + 2^3 + \cdots + 13^3 + 14^3 = $ _____

$1^3 + 2^3 + \cdots + 19^3 + 20^3 = $ _____

Write your rule in words or symbols. _____

_____

POLYCUBES

January 1977

By William J. Masalski, University of Massachusetts, Amherst, MA 01002

Teacher's Guide

Grade level: 7–12

Materials: Cubes made of wood or constructed of heavy stock paper; white glue or rubber cement; graph paper

Objectives: There are many activities involving polyominoes (made from squares). This article on polycubes expands the scope of such activities into three dimensions and aids in the development of insight into the design and construction of the Soma cube and other possible cube puzzles constructed with polycubes.

Directions: Distribute the activity sheets one at a time.

Sheet 1: In finding the tetracubes, have students watch for faces that do not touch fully and for duplications due to repositioning. The eight possible tetracubes are shown on sheet 2.

Sheet 2: A polycube is rectangular if every two points of the solid can be connected by a segment that lies completely within or on the surface of the solid.

One solution to problem 2 is shown in Figure 1.

Sheet 3: Be sure your students know how to use graph paper to sketch the pentacubes accurately. You may want to display a complete set of solutions on the bulletin board, perhaps with each student supplying at least one sketch. The complete set of 29 pentacubes is shown following sheet 3 and can be reproduced and distributed to the class if desired.

Supplementary activity: A very challenging puzzle involves forming a large three-unit cube from three tetracubes (lettered B, F, and G on sheet 2) and three pentacubes (numbered 13, 16, and 18 on the solutions sheet). There are only two known solutions to this problem. One is shown in Figure 2.

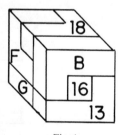

Fig. 1

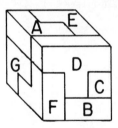

Fig. 2

Editorial comment: The geometric format of this problem-solving activity makes it very suitable for hands-on exploration. Excellent experience can be gained in three-dimensional visualization. Where necessary, help the students along in sketching the first few pentacubes needed for worksheet 3 on graph paper. Once the method is established, the sketching process is greatly simplified. One-centimeter plastic cubes are readily available that can be conveniently interlocked. These can be used effectively to make a complete set of the twenty-nine pentacubes. Symmetries and reflections can be studied in detail with these models.

Polycubes

A polycube is a solid formed from cubes joined completely, face to face. When two unit cubes touch fully along a common face, the resulting solid is called a Bicube.

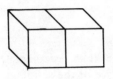

Bicube

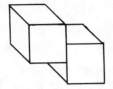

Not a bicube

When three unit cubes are put together so that each cube touches at least one of the other cubes fully along a common face, it is called a Tricube.

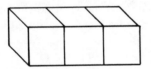

Tricube

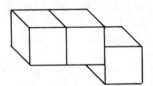

Not a tricube

There are only two different tricubes. Use unit cubes and fasten them together to make rigid models for each.

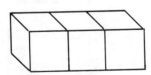

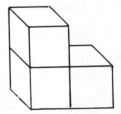

1. A Tetracube is formed from four cubes joined face to face. How many different tetracubes are there? Make a rigid model of each one that you can find. If a tetracube can be flipped or repositioned in such a way that it is exactly like a tetracube already made, then it is not different from the other one.

Polycubes

There are eight possible tetracubes. These eight plus the two possible tricubes (shaded below) can be combined into two groups, rectangular and nonrectangular solids.

Rectangular Solids

Nonrectangular Solids

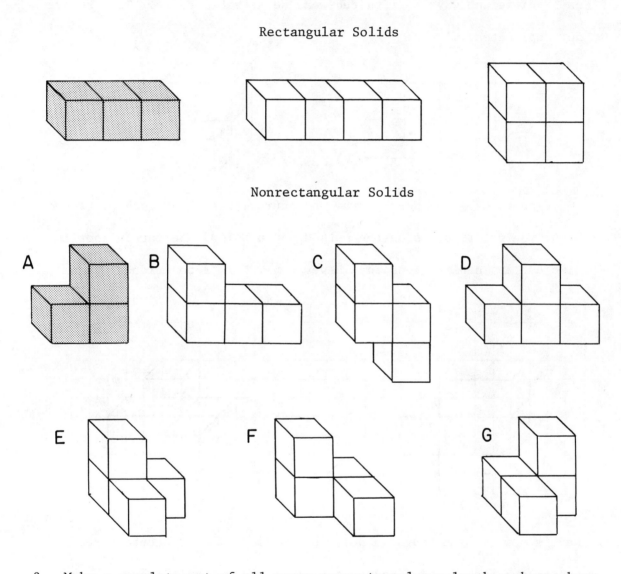

2. Make a complete set of all seven nonrectangular polycubes shown above. Now try to form them into a cube measuring three units on each edge. There are 1 105 920 different ways to do this! How many can you find? This puzzle, originally discovered by Piet Hein, is sold under the name Soma cube.

Polycubes

3. A pentacube is formed from five cubes joined face to face. How many different pentacubes can you find? One systematic way of solving this problem is to take each tetracube and determine how many basically different ways a fifth cube can be attached to it. Then remove any duplicates.

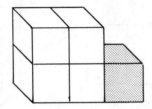
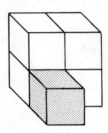

On a sheet of graph paper, draw an accurate sketch of each pentacube that you can find, using the method shown below. Be careful not to include any duplications that have simply been repositioned.

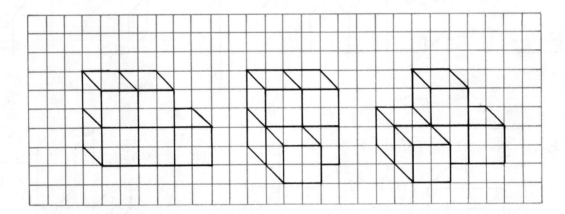

4. Here's how to make your own polycube puzzles. Build a cube three units on a side by placing together twenty-seven unit cubes. From this cube, remove any polycube and glue it together. Continue this process, removing a differently shaped polycube each time and gluing its cubes together. Give the puzzle to some friends. See if they can put it back together to form a cube. Can you?

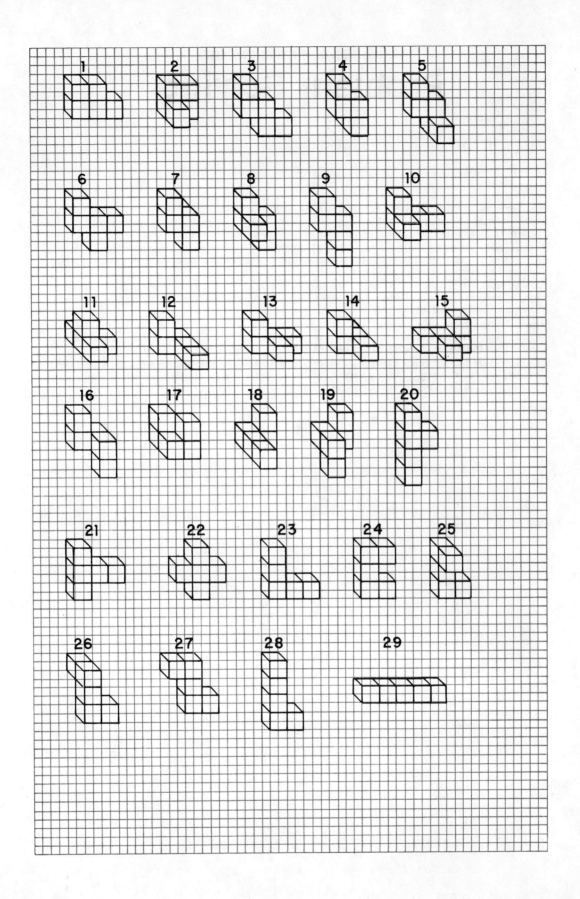

Additional Activities for
Problem Solving

Woolaver, John N. "How Many Blocks in a Triangular Pile?" Oct. 1974, 527–30. Students use spatial visualization to complete a table, an analysis of which leads to the discovery of a pattern that permits prediction of the total number of blocks in a triangular pile of cubes through any given layer. (Grades 7–10)

Hartman, Janet. "Figurate Numbers." Jan. 1976, 47–50. Students draw figures representing triangular, square, and pentagonal numbers; discover patterns generated by differences between consecutive figurate numbers; and use these patterns to predict additional figurate numbers. (Grades 7–10)

Ouellette, Hugh. "Discovery with Number Triangles." Nov. 1978, 678–82. Students discover generalizations involving triangular arrays of numbers called *even triangles, multiple triangles,* and *mixed-up number triangles* by completing tables and searching for patterns. (Grades 7–12)

Bechem, William Jacob. "Pie Packing." Oct. 1979, 519–22. Pupils use properties of 30°-60° right triangles and 45°-45° right triangles to determine the best size of rectangular tray for baking eight or nine pies that are to be held in place by the sides of the tray and by each other. (Grades 8–12)

Bechem, William Jacob. "Tower Trainees." Dec. 1979, 679–82, 700. Students discover patterns, make generalizations, and use a strategy of solving simpler problems in order to solve an adaptation of the classic tower puzzle often called the Tower of Hanoi. (Grades 7–12)